# Avoiding Ditches

## Keeping on the Highway of Balance

*by*

*Dr. Roy Hicks*

# Avoiding Ditches

## Keeping on the Highway of Balance

*by*

*Dr. Roy Hicks*

**Harrison House**
Tulsa, Oklahoma

*Avoiding Ditches*
*Keeping on the Highway of Balance*
ISBN 0-89274-737-4
Copyright © 1995 by Dr. Roy Hicks
1034 La Sombra
San Marcos, CA 92069

Published by Harrison House, Inc.
P.O. Box 35035
Tulsa, OK 74136

# Contents

# About the Author

*by*
*Pastor Steve Overman and Margaret Hicks*

First, by Steve Overman, pastor of Faith Center in Eugene, Oregon:

"As a young pastor of a growing church, I covet the kind of godly, experienced perspective Dr. Hicks has to offer. The issues addressed in this book are timely, and I personally deal with them every day. I found Dr. Hicks' thoughts on them both very enjoyable and very helpful.

"I admire Dr. Hicks and am deeply grateful to him and Margaret for their continuing touch on my life and the larger Church of our Lord. Dr. Hicks is a true Pentecostal patriarch who moves in anointed, incisive teaching and godly guidance garnered from more than fifty years experience in fruitful church ministry."

Then, secondly, who could be better qualified to paint a descriptive, personal portrait of an author than a wife who has lived with him through life's temporary trials and lasting triumphs for fifty years?

"Words characterizing him that immediately come to mind are: singleminded, unswerving, and a man who loves the Word of God . . . and who has an anointed, forthright, no-nonsense presentation of it; one whose entire ministry has been devoted to the study of God's Word and the preaching of its unsearchable riches, with a strong emphasis on faith which he received in early training under the ministry of Aimee Semple McPherson.

"He is a devoted husband, father, and grandfather to his own family and a mentor to countless numbers of young pastors and ministers who look to him (knowing he will not spare them but will instruct them as a father in the faith).

"He is the author of many books, which are designed to be practical, down-to-earth instruction and help for Christians in daily living. Heartwarming testimonies come from people all around the world who have been spiritually benefited by reading them, and I recommend them unreservedly!

"It is my prayer that you will read this book, *Avoiding Ditches,* with an open heart and mind. It will challenge conformist 'tradition for the sake of tradition' thinking; and, I trust, will cause us all to recognize that it is a common enemy, Satan, who keeps us in the ditches of 'extremes' instead of on the highway of balance."

# About the Book

Dear Brother Hicks,

I just finished reading your book, *Avoiding Ditches*. What an extraordinary work in such precise timing for the body of Christ. Your many years of being a student of the Bible certainly manifested as you wrote this knowledge on paper for the rest of us.

Every minister needs this book desperately. In fact, every believer needs to have it at hand as a reference manual for their Christian walk. It's an extremely dark day. If only we would have had books like this twenty years ago, many who are falling away today might have remained solid and stable.

I pray and have my faith with you that this book will saturate the body of Christ and that its title will become a household term. I congratulate you on such precise writing and, as always, hold you in very high esteem.

Your son in the faith,
Mark T. Barclay
Mark Barclay Ministries

# Foreword

I have just finished reading the manuscript for Dr. Roy Hicks' new book. In fact, I read it in one sitting, finding it impossible to put down. This book is a must for every minister of the Gospel.

Unfortunately, the integrity of the modern Charismatic minister in America is in question. The well-publicized moral failures of some leading ministers have hurt our cause, but our doctrinal instability threatens to do far more harm than all the sex and money scandals combined.

If our integrity is to be restored in the eyes of the public, we must be more responsible. We must purpose to turn away from the "winds of doctrine" (Ephesians 4:14) that divide our ranks and weaken our credibility.

On the one hand, "heresy hunters" have gone to the extreme of attacking the positive message of faith in God's Word, slandering wonderful men of God with proven ministries. On the other hand, there are those within our ranks who refuse to defend orthodoxy and think it strife and division when a minister calls for scriptural balance.

Dr. Hicks' book is not an attack on various personalities; it is an attempt to call for balance and stability. It reflects the admonition of the Apostle Paul in 2 Timothy 2:15 calling us to "rightly divide the Word of Truth."

Dr. Hicks is writing from a position of more than fifty years of ministry experience. Clearly, he has no "axe to grind," no religious empire to defend. As I have always known him to be, he simply has a heart for the truth.

May the Spirit of wisdom and revelation guide you as you read these pages.

Willie George

# Introduction

What is wrong with the middle of the road?

Why do we think it is not very safe there? Or perhaps we think it is not very exciting there.

Bible truth must be accepted as always being in the center; therefore, Scripture must be interpreted so that one avoids unbalanced extremes. True Bible doctrine will be found where there is balance.

On each side of our theological road are *ditches.* These are not ordinary, shallow ditches, but deep, dangerous ravines. These are so deep that many of those who have fallen into them on one side or the other of truth do not realize they are in ditches. Thus they can never be rescued from the dangerous depths.

It is a fact that most cults or false religions were founded by people who were members of a traditional Christian church at one time or studied the Bible and Christianity before going astray. We read with dismay some years ago of the deaths of nine hundred people in Guyana, who committed suicide because they believed and followed a cult leader. James Jones at one time was pastor of a Christian church.

A careful study of this kind of extremism usually will show the motivation behind it. The people involved may be good and honest people who are genuine searchers for spiritual things. However, they are moved gradually from belief in the Bible to becoming firm, and even zealous, believers in what their leader says, whether it matches the Bible or not.

The deception usually begins very slowly. In the beginning, perhaps there is only a little *excess* in the leader's beliefs or teachings. Many of the people who follow these leaders come out of churches where the services are dull and uninspiring, while this new leader has great charisma, a magnetic personality, and great preaching ability. He makes going to church exciting.

What he (or she) teaches seems at first to be biblical. It is acceptable, and best of all, it extricates them from what had become a wearisome, religious lifestyle without inspiration. In an eager and enthusiastic frame of mind, they will follow and not even notice as deception creeps in. Now they are on the dangerous path of moving from *followers* to *hero worshippers*.

The absolute loyalty, rapt attention, and devotion of these followers causes the leader to feel he must continue with new and exciting revelations in order not to lose his position or his followers.

In the late Gordon Lindsay's book about a turn-of-the century minister named Alexander Dowie, he uses a word that describes very well how a good man can persuade people to follow him into error through inspired leadership. Lindsay says loyalty to this leader became *a fixation*. The dictionary definition of this word is, "an obsession or preoccupation."

Dowie's dream of building a Christian city that would allow no sin became a fixation with him and his followers. There were to be no dance halls, no gambling houses, no saloons or brothels, no profanity, and so forth. Thousands of good Christians followed him in building Zion, Illinois, endeavoring to help him fulfill this vision.

The end result, however, is that they lost their investments and security, and he eventually lost his leadership, ministry, and his life. The idea may have been *good*, but apparently it was not *God*.

Some ministers have grown to prominence with the best of intentions in serving God, but have been seduced away from their gifts and calling to pursue ventures of faith which God never intended for them to pursue. When a minister (or any believer for that matter) neglects his or her true calling and focuses their time and abilities on other things, they eventually become deceived, fall into error or sin, and some even die prematurely.

Could this happen to you?

Are you such a committed follower of a good man or woman that you accept what is said without doing your own Bible study?

If your leader prophesied in the next service that God was warning all of you to leave America and perhaps flee into South America, would you follow?

Would you empty your wallet and perhaps your bank account because someone teaches that for every dollar you give to his ministry you will get back a hundred percent from the Lord?

Would you send $1,000 to an evangelist who promises healing if you do?

Would you respond to an evangelist who said, "Help me build my city, and you will be healed and prospered?"

Are these things presented by men or women of God moving at the inspiration of the Holy Spirit, or have these things become personal fixations?

I'm not saying God could not specifically give you guidance about moving somewhere or giving to His work through a man or woman of God. However, this kind of guidance should be a *rare exception* to the daily leading of the Spirit in your personal prayer life.

If this sounds too harsh or severe, remember that judgment begins at the house of God, and we must all give an account to Him of our words and actions. Many good Christian people follow ministers who seem better than the average believer and, if they do not study the scriptures for themselves, they will become *hero worshippers*. Most do not realize what has happened until it is too late. Then they tend to blame the leader instead of taking responsibility for their own thoughts and actions.

A good test of a Christian leader or layman is: Will this person receive correction? Will he or she seek advice from reliable people other than those who are staff members or loyal followers? Do they hold themselves accountable to someone who is their elder?

This book is intended to sound a warning. If the body of Christ gets its eyes on an apostle, prophet, evangelist, pastor, or teacher instead of the Lord Himself, and that minister becomes puffed up in the sin of pride, God will eventually allow that minister to fall. He shares His glory with no one.

This is just one of the areas we will be exploring in this book, and I trust that the thoughts expressed will be accepted in the spirit in which they were written: as a heartfelt call to true scriptural balance, one that will ensure that we continue to teach and preach from a foundation of the Word of God, avoiding that which tends toward spiritual trends or fads which tend to "come and go."

The last chapter of this book, "Petitioning," was written by our son, Dr. Roy Hicks Jr., who, soon after finishing it, went to be with the Lord as the result of a plane accident. He wrote from a scholarly position, but also was influenced by the "Jesus Movement" of the 1970s, when the church was challenged to search its collective heart concerning the **faith which was once delivered unto the saints** (Jude 3). He was a continuing student of theology and of the Greek language of the Bible.

We dedicate this book to the memory of our son. He lived and enjoyed life to the fullest, with the Lord Jesus always as the focal point of his life. In his ministry, he never digressed from that goal . . . and steadfastly encouraged all who heard him to be faithful.

He loved his family, but at the same time he had an enduring, fervent longing to go to be with his Lord . . . even referring to it sometimes by saying, "If I should go be with the Lord before you, don't spend too much time thinking about me . . . I probably won't be thinking of you!"

# 1
# Spiritual Gifts

But the manifestation of the Spirit is given to every man to profit withal.

For to one is given by the Spirit the word of wisdom; to another the word of knowledge by the same Spirit;

To another faith by the same Spirit; to another the gifts of healing by the same Spirit;

To another the working of miracles; to another prophecy; to another discerning of spirits; to another divers kinds of tongues; to another the interpretation of tongues.

1 Corinthians 12:7-10

This chapter will deal with the ditches a believer can fall into on either side of the controversial subject of the gifts of the Holy Spirit. On one side, there is the position taken by those who believe the supernatural manifestations of God are not in operation today. On the other side are those who believe in the operation of the gifts as a valid biblical experience, but they have taken their beliefs so far that use of the gifts is abused.

Let us look at the first "ditch." Many denominations and pastors teach their congregations that the Holy Spirit does not exercise His gifts today in the same manner He exercised them the Day of Pentecost. (Acts 2.) Their doctrinal argument is that miracles ceased to be necessary in the Church once we had the written Word, and they base much of this argument on 1 Corinthians 13:8-10:

Charity never faileth: but whether there be prophecies, they shall fail; whether there be tongues,

1

**they shall cease; whether there be knowledge, it shall vanish away.**

**For we know in part, and we prophesy in part.**

**But when that which is perfect is come, then that which is in part shall be done away.**

They believe this passage of Scripture means that because the Church has the Bible, we no longer need the supernatural evidence of God. Therefore, all of the gifts described in 1 Corinthians 12 and the operation of these gifts as discussed in 1 Corinthians 14 are no longer valid for today. In other words, those verses describe past history, not present dealings of the Holy Spirit in the Church.

The Apostle Paul apparently did not have this understanding. Otherwise, if the thirteenth chapter "does away" with the fourteenth, he would have reversed the order of those passages! Actually, if Paul knew the gifts of the Spirit were to "pass away" from the Church, he would never have written the twelfth and fourteenth chapters in the first place.

One of the commentaries written by those who believe this way concedes this point. He says:

That which is perfect cannot be a reference to the completion of the canon of the Scripture; otherwise, we now living in the age of the completed canon would see more clearly than Paul did. Even the most self-satisfied and opinionated of theologians would hardly admit that." [*Wycliffe Bible Commentary*, Chicago: Moody Press, p. 1252.]

In particular, most of the evangelical commentaries on this subject endeavor to spiritualize away prophecy and tongues as not being for today by repeating what Paul wrote in 1 Corinthians 13:8: **They shall fail and cease.**

Readers should take note that the three words mentioned in verse 8 are *prophecy, tongues,* and *knowledge.* Rather than "failing and ceasing," knowledge is on the increase, rapidly adding more knowledge every few months. So we must not yet be at the point where "the perfect" has come and those things are to cease.

Also, many who believe this refers to the supernatural gifts as being "put away," quote 1 Corinthians 13:11: **When I became a man, I put away childish things,** which means baby talk or babyish behavior.

It is absurd to think of the supernatural gifts of the Spirit as ever being "childish things!" Yet many pastors and teachers continue to interpret verse 8 to mean that prophecy and tongues, both belonging to the Holy Spirit and operated by Him, have passed away and are childish notions of the past. They then turn around and, in the same breath, declare that information is still operating today!

Have tongues and prophecy ceased? No! Messages in tongues and prophecy go forth in a great host of Charismatic, Pentecostal, and many denominational churches all around the world each time believers gather together.

Adam Clarke was a Methodist theologian who was not influenced by this Calvinist interpretation that the gifts had ceased when he wrote his Bible commentary. He concluded that *love* is greater than "tongues, prophecy, and knowledge" and that love is the only thing that can fit a soul for the Kingdom of God. [Clarke, Adam. *Commentary on the Bible*, Nashville: Abingdon and Cokesbury; Vol. 6, p. 270.]

The first thing we need to see here is that the subject and focus of 1 Corinthians 13 is love. It is not about spiritual gifts at all, but merely mentions them in comparison to love. The whole message of this chapter is that everything we do, even operating in the gifts, must be motivated by love.

Verse 12b says:

> **Now I know in part, but *then* I shall know even as also I am known.**

Even a layperson can understand that tongues, prophecy, and knowledge shall cease when *then* (future tense) comes, and we *shall* know as we are known. That means *in Heaven*.

I recall a conversation with a former denominational pastor who had been baptized in the Holy Spirit. When I asked him, "How could you, a pastor educated in a seminary, read the fourteenth chapter of 1 Corinthians and believe that the Apostle Paul was against praying in tongues?"

He laughed and said, "I never *read* it," meaning that when he read it, he "read" with unseeing eyes, because he already had made up his mind on the subject. He saw what he believed, not what was really on the page.

Anyone can twist scriptures to fit preconceived ideas and traditional doctrines. What an awesome responsibility preachers have to be honest with what the Bible really says!

In my opinion, this ditch serves to rob today's Christian of the option to covet the best gifts of the Holy Spirit (1 Corinthians 12:31) and operate in those gifts. It makes God a respecter of persons by saying that the gifts were viable at one time for one generation of the Church, but not at this time for our generation of the Church. Thus, many believers are denied the blessings of God and deeper intimacy with God because they walk in this ditch.

## The Other Ditch

Now let us examine the practices of those who have found themselves in a ditch on the other side by abusing the gifts of the Spirit. In most cases, their spiritual leaders were not governed by scriptural teaching, and they allowed their congregations to operate in the gifts of the Spirit whenever and however they choose. They do not exercise the spiritual authority or fulfill the responsibility that goes with their offices.

The vocal gifts are the ones most often abused:

1. The gift of divers kinds of tongues
2. The gift of interpretation of tongues
3. The gift of prophecy
4. The gift of the word of wisdom
5. The gift of the word of knowledge

Pastors who allow the gifts to be operated without any oversight will have many manifestations surfacing in their services that are not truly from the Holy Spirit. Such displays, usually by untaught Christians, will embarrass the Church. Visitors exposed to this sort of behavior will seldom return.

The regrettable outcome of this is that, as a result of these unbridled actions, many pastors will stop all exercise of the gifts and thus hinder or stop altogether the moving of the Holy Spirit in their churches.

When this happens, the services become dull and lifeless, and the pastor might as well take down the sign that proclaims that church is "full-gospel," Pentecostal, or Charismatic. I have friends who have not only said "no" to the exercise of the gifts of the Spirit but have severely cut back on the amount of praise and worship as well.

If God had not wanted everyone to speak in tongues, He would not have poured out His precious Holy Spirit on the Day of Pentecost. Also, He would not have brought renewal in the early 1900s at Stone's House in Topeka, Kansas, and Azusa Street in Los Angeles, California. Nor would we have had the mighty renewal of the operation of the gifts that has occurred over the past two decades. All of the moves mentioned in this paragraph have been accompanied by speaking in tongues and have had all of the nine gifts of the Spirit manifested in them.

This book is not being written to say to those who do not speak in tongues, "Do as we do," but neither is it written to say to those who do speak in tongues, "Stop coveting and operating in the gifts of the Spirit." I do pray that it will cause believers to re-examine what it is that motivates us to have the kind of services we have in our churches.

What a retreat from the Scripture it is when a church, either because of doctrinal error or with good intentions to stop abuses of the operation of the gifts of the Holy Spirit, refuses to allow Him to move in this way in their services. God never intended for miracles and supernatural manifestations to cease. The nine gifts of the Holy Spirit are for today. However, we must follow faithfully the firm guidelines of the authority given to us in 1 Corinthians 14.

In some churches, anyone at any time is allowed to exercise what they believe to be one of the gifts, especially the vocal ones. Pastors who try to follow this course simply because it has always been done that way in their denomination find themselves lacking in authority and up to their eyeballs in confusion.

After more than fifty years of witnessing the exercise of the gifts of the Holy Spirit in public services, I would like to suggest some guidelines that could profit all who use them.

## Guidelines for Ministry in the Gifts

The first guideline is a practical one, serving to minimize distracting movement in the congregation as much as possible. Pastors who do not permit people to get up and disturb the service while a word is being given or the Word is being taught are walking in their God-given authority. (Ecclesiastes 5:1.)

Once, as guest speaker in a church that I had never visited before, the pastor asked me if I had any suggestions or if I would give him my impression of his church. I replied that after just one night it would be difficult to assess his church; however, I said that there did seem to be a lot of moving around. His immediate reply was, "No, I don't think they move around very much."

The next night he and his wife seated themselves where they could observe the congregation while I was speaking. Apparently this restlessness and moving around had come to pass progressively over the years, because he had not noticed it. He was shocked at how much movement there was, and he scolded his congregation soundly.

I have noticed this as being one of the factors that discourages growth, especially in smaller churches. Whenever someone moves around, it distracts people from hearing the precious Word of God. Those who are hungry to hear will be frustrated.

The second guideline for the pastor is to see that the vocal gifts are operated decently and in order. In many churches, anyone at any time can give a message in tongues and prophesy. Where this is allowed, you may be sure there is no understanding of 1 Corinthians 14.

In that chapter, the Apostle Paul laid down a number of principles for the Corinthian church to follow. It is obvious that control must be exercised by the pastor for the service to be held "decently and in order," as Paul instructed in verse 40. It is important, however, that guidelines or rules must not be enforced before the people in the church understand them thoroughly.

*Decently* is translated from a Greek word that means "honestly," and *in order* from a Greek word that means "regular arrangement, i.e., (in time) fixed succession (of rank, or character), official dignity." [Strong, James. *The New Strong's Exhaustive Concordance of the Bible* (Nashville: Thomas Nelson Inc., 1991), "Greek Dictionary," #2156, p. 34, #5010, p. 70.]

With regard to *order,* the pastor should first teach on the gifts of the Spirit in several services. People should understand the authority and responsibility God has placed on the pastor in overseeing and monitoring the operation of the gifts during a service.

It is best to allow a specific time for the moving of God's Spirit, but it should be understood that although services are preplanned, the pastor will allow the Holy Spirit to move at any time He wills. I believe the pastor, sensing the Spirit's desire to speak, should say something brief like: "Every head bowed before the Lord. I believe we are to hear from God. Please do not speak until you are recognized and receive permission. If you feel you have a word for us, please raise your hand."

Usually more than one hand will be raised, and the pastor or someone to whom he has delegated that responsibility must get a witness from the Holy Spirit concerning who to call upon. Rarely will visitors be given permission to speak, simply because they are not known and it is uncertain whether they are really operating in the Holy Spirit. Pastors have a charge to protect their flocks from false prophets and false operation of gifts, as well as false doctrines.

There are times when someone has been given permission to speak, but after a few statements, the pastor realizes the word being given is not from God. It could either be unscriptural or condemning. At these times, he has the responsibility to stop the speaker and, if necessary, explain why to the people.

We have also known of churches where a certain elder has been designated by the pastor as the one to be approached if a member has something to share. The elder then gives the note or a list to the pastor, and the person or persons may be called on at the proper time. The flow of the service can continue without interruption.

Many large churches have solved the problem of the people's inability to hear because of the great size of the sanctuary by setting up microphones in the altar space. I am invited to churches whose congregations number in the thousands and this provision has enabled them to be blessed by the operation of the gifts. The availability of microphones has given "official dignity" to this important segment of the service.

The Holy Spirit can function more easily and effectively where there is control and order. There is a right time for all good things to occur, and there is a wrong time, and He will lead the pastor in this determination.

Jesus was amazed at the centurion's faith because, from a secular sense, he not only understood authority himself, but recognized that the Lord Jesus also ministered with authority because He himself was *under* authority. Therefore, we can see that where there is no authority, there can be no real ministry.

The pastor should exercise his God-given authority over every aspect of the service, including the length of the singing and worship and the operation of the gifts of the Spirit. Not only does this make the Holy Spirit feel welcome, but it gives security to the congregation. They know their pastor will listen to the Spirit and act accordingly to protect them from false teaching and false prophets.

It would be far wiser to permit some manifestation of the gifts, even through those who could be termed weak or inexperienced, as opposed to grieving the Holy Spirit by not allowing the operation of any gifts at all. Encourage those who are beginning to operate in the gifts to "practice" in the beginning during mid-week services, which usually are smaller and not so intimidating to a novice.

I urge pastors to allow spiritual gifts to operate in their services and encourage those who already allow the gifts to be operated to be sure they maintain the authority necessary to keep the services decent and orderly.

## The Gifts Are To Build Up the Church

In the fourteenth chapter of 1 Corinthians, the Apostle Paul gave some very important instructions regarding the operation of the gifts of the Spirit:

1. The gifts seek to edify (build up) the Church, the corporate Body of Christ, not the individual. (v. 3,4.) This is not for direction of personal affairs, such as marriage, ministry call, missionary call, or to correct leadership, but is intended to benefit the whole Church.

2. If you speak in tongues, you should pray to be able to interpret what you are saying. (v. 5-13.) This is referring to the gift of tongues, where the Holy Spirit speaks to an entire congregation. Obviously, if it is not interpreted, it is of no benefit to anyone, because no one understands it.

3. When the local church meets, there should be no more than three vocal messages, with the understanding that a tongue and interpretation of that tongue is equal to prophecy. (v. 27, 29.)

4. If no interpreter is present, the person with a message in tongues should remain silent. (v. 28.)

5. The "spirit of the prophet is subject to the prophet" means a person with a message from God can wait his turn or wait on the Lord's timing. (v.32, 33.)

6. Paul wrote that we should "covet" to prophesy. In other words, we are to covet to "bring enlightenment" to all. (v. 39.)

7. Paul said not to forbid speaking with tongues. (v. 39.) Many churches never encourage tongues and interpretation of tongues in their services. Not encouraging this is the same or has the effect of forbidding anyone to speak with tongues in public.

# Instructions for the Individual

Most saints of God not only receive help and blessing in hearing the gifts in a public service but have a desire stirred within them to be vessels for the operation of these wonderful gifts. If you, dear reader, are one of these who are hungry for a greater spiritual experience and greater depth in the Lord, here are some instructions that will help you.

Do not *try* to be used, just allow yourself to be open for the use of the Holy Spirit. If you believe you have a word to give but are not quite sure, here are some ways to find out if this is really the Holy Spirit moving on you:

1. Ask the Holy Spirit to keep impressing you with the message.

2. Take authority over Satan in Jesus' name, so no demonic spirit will be able to speak to you.

3. Make sure your heart is right with God and your relationships with others are right.

4. Do not have an "axe to grind," some agenda of your own to put forward.

5. Do not get carried away and end up trying to preach.

6. Do not continue after the Holy Spirit is finished.

7. Do not be condemnatory.

8. Do not speak too long in either tongue or prophecy. It is better for the listeners to remember one or two things than to give up because there is too much to recall.

9. Avoid excessive loudness.

10. Do not say, "Thus saith the Lord," unless you are absolutely certain it is the Lord giving you the message through the Holy Spirit.

This chapter has not been written to describe each individual gift of the Holy Spirit in depth, but has focused on the vocal gifts. As I said earlier, they are the ones most misunderstood and abused. However, if you are interested, there are many good and informative books about all nine gifts in Christian bookstores.

# General Guidelines

**For as many as are led by the Spirit of God, they are the sons of God.**

**Romans 8:14**

The Holy Spirit within you wants to direct your life, and He will take of the things of Jesus and reveal them to you. (John 16:14,15.) Therefore, being led solely by someone's prophecy cannot only be dangerous but can grieve the Holy Spirit within you.

When a prophecy comes forth and it seems to speak directly to you or a situation you are facing, take comfort, but ask the Holy Spirit within you to lead you and guide you concerning it.

**Quench not the Spirit. Despise not prophesyings.**
**1 Thessalonians 5:19,20**

May we always seek to honor the precious Holy Spirit and His ministry. May we not quench or grieve Him or despise His gifts!

Under the Old Covenant, when the Holy Spirit left a person they did not know it. Samson did not know the Holy Spirit had left him. (Judges 16:20.) If it is also possible for this to happen under the New Covenant, then we have an even greater responsibility not to grieve Him.

The names of many people come to mind as I think of this. They are Spirit-filled ministers who, at one time, had great and effectual ministries, but their lives ended in defeat and tragedy because they grieved the Holy Spirit too many times.

I exhort you to search your heart continually and always be ready to repent. Be very sensitive to the Holy Spirit, the blessed Third Person of the Trinity, and honor His ministry *and* gifts.

# 2

# The Trinity

Whether or not there *is* a "Trinity" has been fervently debated ever since the days of the early Church.On one side, we have those in the ancient ditch who believe there is only *one* God. The Jews still believe this and will not change as a nation until they see the revealed Christ.

In another deep but extreme ditch are the "Jesus Only" groups who believe that God came to earth as Jesus, and He is the only Deity we will see throughout eternity.

Then there is a third teaching that Jesus *laid aside His deity when He came to earth* and lived out His thirty-three years as only a man.

Let us begin by establishing that God, from the beginning, was *one* God, but a "triune" Being. The original Hebrew word translated "God" in English is *Elohim.* That is a plural form of God, meaning more than one. There would not seem to be a successful argument against this truth, yet controversy continues.

An eminent Jewish rabbi, Simeon ben Joachi said:

Come and see the mystery of the word *Elohim;* there are three degrees, and each degree by itself along, and yet notwithstanding, they are all one and joined together in one, and are not divided from each other. [*Adam Clarke Commentary*, Vol. 1, p. 28.]

In Genesis 1:26, where Moses first wrote of God's idea of creating man, *Elohim* is used and is translated in the plural. Its use in this verse seems to indicate that there was perfect unity in the Trinity even at the time when Adam was created.

**And God** (Elohim) **said, Let us make man in our image, after our likeness.**

*Elohim* also is used in Genesis 3:22, 11:7, 21:7and 53. Other reference works that explain the use of this word are *Strong's Concordance* [#430, p. 12] and Adam Clarke in his commentary on the Bible. Clarke said of the meaning of Elohim:

"Infinitely perfect, and infinitely happy, because infinitely and eternally self-sufficient and *needing nothing that He has made.*" [Clarke, Vol. 1, p. 27.]

In my opinion, to say there is not a Trinity but only one person in the Godhead ignores many passages of Scripture. Jesus frequently addressed the Father; on several occasions the Father answered Him or spoke to Him and was heard by many people; and Jesus spoke often of the Holy Spirit, the Comforter He would send to live in believers after He ascended to His Father in heaven — all which could not be possible if there were only one person in the Godhead.

Let's examine the teaching that Jesus was only a man on this earth. Those who believe this teach that Jesus became the "last Adam" in order to redeem us from the mistakes of the "first Adam," thus justifying their teaching that He was all man, not "all man and all God," as the Church has taught and believed for hundreds of years. However, the Apostle Paul wrote:

**And so it is written, The first man Adam was made a living soul; the last Adam was made a quickening spirit.**
**1 Corinthians 15:45**

There is a difference between a living soul and a quickening spirit. A living soul is merely a human being, but a quickening spirit is One Who gives eternal life to others. Only God in man could have that capability. There are other scriptures which also reveal that Jesus was both God and man in one person while on earth — not *just* God nor *just* man. For example, in John 1:1 and 14:

> **In the beginning was the Word, and the Word was with God, and the Word was God.**

> **And the Word was made flesh, and dwelt among us, (and we beheld his glory, the glory as of the only begotten of the Father,) full of grace and truth.**

The Bible leaves no doubt that Jesus walked this earth as all God and all man. He had to lay aside His glory and take upon Himself a human body; otherwise, He could not have died for the sins of the world. However, He did not lay aside His divinity.

There is another belief in existence that Jesus was always *only* man, never God. This teaching goes even farther than the doctrine that Jesus was God who laid aside deity to become man and makes Him out to be a man like all other men. This belief appears mostly among the cults. *It is the one thing on which all cults seem to agree.*

The Apostle John wrote that we should "try" or test the spirits to see whether they are of God, which means we also should try teachings, doctrines, and the fruits of these things to determine truth. Truth is found in the Word of God, the real standard or measuring stick for everything.

> **Beloved, believe not every spirit, but try the spirits whether they are of God: because many false prophets are gone out into the world.**

> **Hereby know ye the Spirit of God: Every spirit that**

> **confesseth that Jesus Christ is come in the flesh is of God:**

**And every spirit that confesseth not that Jesus Christ has come in the flesh is not of God: and this is that spirit of antichrist, whereof ye have heard that it should come; and even now already is in the world.**
**1 John 4:1-3**

The incarnation ("come in the flesh," perfect tense) implies the eternal nature of His deity. In other words, Jesus' deity was always with Him — before, during and after He became a man. Christian theologians tell us that this verse simply means that if anyone teaches that Jesus Christ lived on this earth as mere man, it is the spirit of antichrist.

I recall an incident that happened while I was pastoring in the Midwest some years ago. One of our church members brought her sister to a service. She had forewarned me that the sister was a spiritualist (one who talks with spirits and/or allows spirits to talk through them). So I took especial note of the sister's responses to the service.

The two ladies had made an appointment with my wife and myself after the service concluded, during which I asked the sister which part of the service she most enjoyed. She said, "All of it."

I questioned her further about the music, as we had sung songs dealing with the blood of Jesus, and she responded, "We use many of those same songs in our services."

But when I asked her if spiritualists believed that Jesus Christ came in the flesh, I was not fully prepared for the change that came over her. She recoiled as if I had struck her and said, "Oh, no! We do not believe that!"

One of the arguments for Jesus having only been man on earth says that Jesus was just another one of the prophets. But Philippians 2:6 says that Jesus **being in the form of God, thought it not robbery to be equal with God.**

That means Jesus was equal to God in the Godhead (the Trinity), but limited Himself to an earthly body of flesh for a season, which is why He said, "The Father is greater than I." Pastor Coleman Phillips says, *"He emptied Himself of His prerogatives of duty, but not of His essentials of Deity."*

In 1 Timothy 3:16 the Word of God teaches that **God was manifest in the flesh.** If Jesus was not God, His entire life, as well as his death, was a lie. He was crucified because He claimed to be the Son of God and the Son of Man. (See Matthew 26:63-66; Luke 20:41-44, Luke 22:69-71; and John 10:36.)

Jesus could not have died on the cross for our sins as a mere human being, because He said His life could not be taken from Him. He declared He laid down His life of His own will in John 10:18. Here are some other reasons in the Bible why Jesus was God as well as man:

• While here on earth, Jesus received praise and worship, which is the just due of God but not of man. (See Matt. 8:2, 9:18, 14:33, and 28:9; Luke 19:37,40; Mark 5:6.)

• Jesus was called the "Lord of Glory" while He was on earth. (1 Corinthians 2:8.)

• Jesus was known by Satan and the demons of hell before He came to earth, and they knew Him to be *more* than mortal man while He was on earth. (Matthew 4:8; Mark 5:7.)

• Standing at the River Jordan, Jesus was identified by God, from *heaven,* as His Son. (Matthew 3:17,17:5.)

• Jesus confounded the most intelligent and informed leaders of His day in the temple at Jerusalem when He was only twelve years of age. When His parents questioned Him as to why He had not started home to Nazareth with them, He asked them if they were not aware that He must be about His Father's business? (Luke 2:42-51.) He knew this from birth, not by the anointing that was to come later.

I was surprised to hear a Charismatic minister on television not long ago explain that while Jesus was here on earth He was not God. This man used Hebrews 2:10 and 5:8 as the basis for his teachings, saying that Jesus could not have been *made perfect* as those verses say if He already was God, because God cannot be perfected. But to what kind of perfection was the writer of Hebrews referring?

In Luke 13:32, Jesus said that on the third day (when He rose from the dead) He would be *perfected.* W.E. Vine says it best: (This is speaking) "of Christ's assured completion of His earthly course, in the accomplishment of the Father's will, the successive stages culminating in His death." [*Vine's Expository Dictionary of Old and New Testament Words* (New York: Fleming H. Revell Co., 1981), Vol. 3, p. 174.]

This does not mean that Jesus was not God in His earthly body, but it means *the human part of Him must learn how to suffer.* The Son of Man, seed of David, had never before in eternity suffered, because the sins of mankind had not been previously placed on Him. [Clarke's *Commentary,* Vol. 5, p. 698.]

When Jesus was in the Garden of Gethsemane the night before He was crucified, He prayed as a man becoming a sacrificial lamb and facing the horrible death of crucifixion. He prayed, **Not as I will, but as You will** (Matthew 26:39 NKJV). He learned as a man and became perfected as a man to become a perfect sacrifice. He did not need to learn moral perfection. It would be close to blasphemy to say that.

I think you can see from the body of Scripture presented here that Jesus was all man and all God. Some perceive the divine Trinity's earthly assignments as being less sovereign in nature. But God gives us a clear warning not to make the mistake of trivializing any assignment of any member of the Trinity.

And whosoever speaketh a word against the Son of
man, it shall be forgiven him: but whosoever speaketh
against the Holy Ghost, it shall not be forgiven him,
neither in this world, neither in the world to come.
**Matthew 12:32**

Most of the twelfth chapter of Matthew is a warning
about taking the deity away from the Lord Jesus while He
was on earth, but there was an even stronger warning about
speaking against the Holy Spirit. In addition to the
"ditches" on the deity of Jesus, there are those who do not
believe in the Holy Spirit.

# Grieving the Holy Spirit

The Apostle Paul warned, in Ephesians 4:30, **And
grieve not the holy Spirit of God whereby ye are sealed
unto the day of redemption**. In 1 Thessalonians 5:19, he
wrote **Quench not the Spirit**. The Holy Spirit's personality
is likened to that of a dove, the most sensitive of all birds.
This means the Holy Spirit is keenly aware of careless and
often heedless treatment.

Let's first look at the important functions of the Holy
Spirit. One of His most important assignments is to take the
things of Jesus and show them to us.

"**Nevertheless I tell you the truth. It is to your
advantage that I go away; for if I do not go not away, the
Helper will not come to you; but if I depart, I will send
Him to you.**

"**And when He has come, He will convict the world
of sin, and of righteousness, and of judgment:**

"**of sin, because they do not believe in me;**

"**of righteousness, because I go to My Father, and
you see Me no more;**

"**of judgment, because the ruler of this world is
judged.**

"I still have many things to say to you, but you cannot bear them now.

"However, when He, the Spirit of truth, has come, He will guide you into all truth: for He will not speak on His own authority; but whatever He hears He will speak; and He will tell you things to come.

"He will glorify Me: for He will take of what is Mine and declare it to you.

"All things that the Father has are Mine. Therefore, I said that He will take of Mine and declare it to you.

"A little while, and you will not see Me; and again a little while, and you will see Me, because I go to the Father."

**John 16:7-16 NKJV**

Please notice that the ministry of the Holy Spirit is here on earth and has been since the Day of Pentecost. (Acts 2.) He is the One who makes Jesus real to us in our hearts. (That is why a believer will say, "Jesus lives in me.") We get everything through and by the Holy Spirit, who also is God.

According to Matthew 12:32, knowingly and maliciously attributing the works of the Holy Spirit to the devil is immediately unforgivable. By grieving or quenching His ministry continuously, you will cause Him to cease ministering the things of Jesus to you.

Quenching the Holy Spirit is taught as a continuing action in Scripture, which infers that judgment may not always be immediate. Here are a few actions that might quench or grieve the Holy Spirit:

1. Exalting Him instead of Jesus. (See John 15:26 and 16:13,14.)

2. Asking Him for things pertaining to the earthly kingdom instead of going to Jesus, who is the appointed sovereign head of the Church.

3. Speaking words as "prophecy" or as a "word of knowledge," when they come from your own carnal mind or wounded spirit.

4. Prophesying events that do not come to pass without later acknowledging the error. If someone who makes an inaccurate prophecy would later acknowledge it, this would help preserve the integrity of the ministry. Do not ever say, "Thus saith the Lord," unless you *know* for sure it truly comes from Him.

All of the above are "ditches" of misapplication of Scripture and carry with them strong penalties. May God help us to be scrupulously careful in the way we handle the precious Word of God and the work of the Holy Spirit.

Many Christians have difficulty discerning between the working of God's Holy Spirit and the working of a familiar spirit (a demon). But there is one sure way to tell whether the Holy Spirit or a demon is running a service. The Holy Spirit only honors and exalts Jesus. If the ministry going forth does not honor and exalt Jesus, then the Holy Spirit will withdraw.

When the Holy Spirit departs, many ministers meet their following's demand to produce the supernatural by moving in their own mind and flesh instead of seeking God. At this point, they open the door to familiar spirits. If the Holy Spirit withdraws from a person, a ministry, a church, or even a service, familiar spirits have a legal right to move in. If that happens, even the most dedicated believers may be deceived.

Many Christians follow these types of ministers. They end up in the ditch, running all over the country following signs and wonders, not Jesus. A good, solid church where they can worship, fellowship with the saints, and be taught sound doctrine from the Bible would be infinitely more helpful to them. God is not "over there" in greener pastures. He is "right there" with them where they are.

A Christian will find it very difficult to stay out of the ditches mentioned in this chapter if he does not have an understanding of the Godhead — the Trinity — and the assignments of each member of the Trinity.

# Divine Assignments of the Trinity

Jesus Christ was the Creator of all things (John 1:1-4), and He also is upholding (sustaining) all things by the Word of His power. (Hebrews 1:2,3; Colossians 1:16.)

God the Father loves the world; however, He will love people with a *parental* love and have a personal relationship with them only as they believe in and love His Son, Jesus. (John 16:27.) He is to be worshipped. (John 4:23,24.) He can be approached by all of His children, to give them the things they ask for in the name of Jesus. (Matthew 6:33, 18:19; John 16:24,25.)

The Holy Spirit is to live within us and teach, comfort, counsel, and empower us. He will reveal *Jesus* and make *Him* real to us as we pray in the same manner as the apostles and the disciples prayed. (Ephesians 1:16-23, 3:14-21).

# Unity in the Trinity

**Nevertheless, when everything has been made subject to God, then shall the Son Himself be subject to God, who gave Him power over all things. Thus, in the end, shall God be wholly and absolutely God.**

**1 Corinthians 15:28 (Phillips)**

It seems that the Godhead will not be totally and finally united as One *as They were in the beginning* until Jesus destroys the last enemy to be destroyed: death. At that time, He will present both Himself and the Church to the Father, that God "may be all in all."

At that time the end will come, when Christ, having abolished all other rule, authority, and power, will hand the Kingdom of God to the Father. Christ's reign will and must continue until every enemy has been conquered.

How can we fully understand this? We cannot. But perhaps the following explanations will assist your faith in trying to grasp this magnificent truth.

We have seen that the Hebrew word for God, *Elohim*, is plural, which means that God is more than a single deity. When it was necessary to redeem man, Jesus was the member of the Trinity to offer Himself as a sacrifice for the sins of the world.

> **Therefore, when He came into the world, He said:**
> **"Sacrifice and offering You did not desire,**
> **But a body You have prepared for Me.**
> **In burnt offerings and sacrifice for sin**
> **You had no pleasure.**
> **Then I said, 'Behold, I have come —**
> **In the volume of the book it is written of Me —**
> **To do Your will, O God.'"**
>
> **Previously saying, "Sacrifice and offering, burnt offerings, and offerings for sin You did not desire, nor had pleasure in them" (which are offered according to the law),**
>
> **then He said, "Behold, I have come to do Your will, O God." He takes away the first that He may establish the second.**
>
> **By that will we have been sanctified through the offering of the body of Jesus Christ once for all.**
> **Hebrews 10:5-10 NKJV**

The entire story of redemption from Genesis to Revelation is the result of Elohim, the Trinity, redeeming mankind. Elohim is separate only in assignments, i.e., appointing Jesus to become the earthly voice and physical manifestation of the Godhead.

Redemption is given totally to our Lord Jesus and will be given back to God the Father after that total redemption is complete and the last enemy, death, is destroyed.

## Understanding the Trinity

Perhaps Adam Clarke [Vol. 6, p. 600] stated the complexity of the Trinity best by saying:

> "This is part of the mystery of godliness which, while we have every reasonable evidence to believe, we have not the power to comprehend."

Our natural minds have great difficulty comprehending the Godhead. Even though the Bible makes it clear that there are three members, it also makes it equally clear that they are one at all times and in all places.

It is important for Christians to have an understanding of the Trinity, not only because it is part of the Bible, but because they can more ably defend the faith and keep themselves out of the ditches of false doctrine and even cults.

# 3
# Faith

Throughout the years of Church history, various great Bible truths have diminished at times and almost disappeared because of lack of proper teaching from the pulpit. At one time or another, this was true of exercising the vocal gifts of the Holy Spirit, worshipping the Lord, speaking with tongues, ministry to the needy, and the duty to participate in civil government, or our political responsibilities as citizens.

Historically, when the Church became aware of the neglect of the above-mentioned teachings and others, there was a flurry on everyone's part to correct the imbalance. What usually happened was that we pulled ourselves out of the ditch of doctrinal neglect with such zeal that we ended up in the ditch on the other extreme.

A great truth which had been neglected for years was that of the "faith message." Simply put, the faith message is that God is a good God who wants you to prosper in all areas of your life. You do this by renewing the mind with His promises, believing them, confessing them, and expecting them to manifest in your life.

When I first came into Pentecostal circles in the 1930s, there seemed to be a great uncertainty or fear that if one dressed nicely or drove a nice car, he would place himself in danger of being considered either prideful or in sin.

Also during those years, there seemed to be confusion as to whether or not it was God's perfect will to be healed in every case and to live in health. These doubts and uncertainties as to the will of God served to make the majority of Christians appear very negative. It was rare to meet a person of positive faith.

Those who believed and endeavored to live strong in faith many times were actually considered to be verging on Christian Science beliefs.

During the 1940s, I sat under the ministry of the late Aimee Semple McPherson, a woman who was one of the greatest evangelists of this century. She was a very positive and persuasive minister of the Gospel. She believed in and preached faith, prayer, and the prosperity of the saints. I was greatly influenced by this.

I also read much about the late Smith Wigglesworth, who was a renowned English evangelist, and of other great men and women of God who successfully ministered the message of faith.

What I read in the Word of God, coupled with the exploits of the great ministries which I had read about, served to encourage me to preach the message of faith. Being young and just out of Bible college, I was not prepared for the reactions of some older, more experienced Pentecostal pastors. These men "judged" me as having been influenced by Christian Science teaching!

I am thankful to God today that, in spite of all the criticism and opposition, I never wavered in those early days, but I continued to preach in a very positive way that God *is* a good God who does not want to see His people sick or in want.

The message of faith relating to divine healing was revived during the late 1940s and 1950s through many healing evangelists, who held large tent and civic auditorium meetings. Then a new sound of revival began to be heard in some areas of the world during the late 1960s and in the 1970s. A wave of revival among "street people" known as "hippies" began on the West Coast of the United States. Simultaneously, God began a sovereign move of the

Holy Spirit among the Roman Catholics and Protestant denominations that previously excluded the Pentecostal experience.

Out of this revival, called the Charismatic movement, came large churches of several thousand members. Christian television programs became popular, Christian networks were established, and many people were saved and filled with the Holy Spirit in those years.

About the same time, a renewed emphasis was being placed on the message that "God is a *good* God," and that He wants His people to be blessed in health and finances just as John the Beloved wrote to Gaius in 3 John 2 (Wuest):

> **Beloved, in all things I am praying that you will be prospering, and that you will be continually having good health just as your soul is prospering.**

Those years were a season of tremendous victory and joy; however, even then I observed the beginnings of imbalance and was prompted to write a book endeavoring to restore balance in this area. Hopefully, *Praying Beyond God's Ability*, helped to serve in counteracting the imbalance to a certain extent.

## Reception of the "Faith Message"

Faith preachers and teachers began to appear in greater numbers than ever before. It was evident that many began to teach with no pastoral experience or training in theology.

Jack Hayford, pastor of Church on the Way in Los Angeles, once wisely admonished a young evangelist, "If you had ever pastored, you would not be saying some of the things you are saying."

There suddenly seemed to be an overabundance of the message that God wants us to be healthy and prosperous. Scripture was used and taught only as a means to meeting personal needs. Prosperity was taught to the extent that, if you were not living in the "best" house or driving the "best" car, perhaps your faith was not the "best" faith!

What had happened? The Church had gone right over the middle again and had fallen into the ditch on the other side. From not believing in health and financial prosperity, we had gone to the extreme of measuring faith by prosperity.

This imbalance has seemed to drive a great majority of Pentecostals back to the previous ditch of not believing in the "faith message." This is regrettable, because the message is the same Word of God that always has been in Scripture.

Finding ourselves in these ditches seems to be the result of *overreacting* to excess, which drives whatever balance is there to a position of imbalance. Which is worse — *to be overzealous and go too far or to retreat from scriptural teaching altogether?*

As a young pastor, I endeavored to teach faith as the Apostle Paul taught it, particularly in the "grace-and-faith" book of Romans. There never was any criticism from the people in my congregations. Rather, there was a hunger in their hearts for this positive Word. In all of the five churches which I pastored and taught this message, not one failed to have steady growth.

Many years later, after I was no longer a pastor but in an official capacity in my denomination, I did begin to hear such statements as: "I don't like the word *confession*. Can't you use a better word? This came from a fellow minister in my denomination. I said, "Certainly — if you can *find a better* biblical word!"

Then, in my travels and from other sources, I began to hear such statements as, "That kind of teaching could put the saints under guilt and condemnation if they have what some would consider a failure." My answer was and is, "If you are believing God to heal you through surgery or if you have to borrow money to do what He's led you to do, go ahead. There is no condemnation in Christ."

People in the churches I pastored were never made to feel guilty for using whatever aid was available. The devil never invented or provided mankind with anything that ministered help or comfort. All good gifts are from above and come from God (James 1:17) and He uses natural things to prosper us more as well as miracles.

There has arisen a tumult of opposition against faith teachers in the past ten years. To determine whether or not this opposition is deserved, let us examine what the Apostle Paul wrote about the kind of faith he preached and taught wherever he travelled.

## Paul's Teachings on Faith

Paul made it crystal clear that every believer has an ample measure of faith in Romans 12:3. In Romans 10:8-10, he told us exactly how faith has to work in order to receive what is desired from the Lord:

> **The word is nigh thee, even in thy mouth, and in thy heart: that is, the word of faith, which we preach;**
>
> **That if thou shalt confess with thy mouth the Lord Jesus, and shalt believe in thine heart that God hath raised him from the dead, thou shalt be saved.**
>
> **For with the heart man believeth unto righteousness; and with the mouth confession is made unto salvation.**

The greatest miracle you will ever receive is yours when you confess (with your mouth) and believe (in your heart) that Jesus died for you and was raised from the dead. That miracle is salvation. When you become born again, you have been saved from sin and from the curse of the results of sin.

The word *saved* is the Greek word *sozo*, which means "to save, deliver, protect, heal, preserve, and make whole." [*Strong's Concordance*, "Greek Dictionary," #4982, p. 70.] If there were no other proof that divine healing is in the atonement provided by Jesus through His work on the cross, the word *sozo* would be sufficient evidence.

Some theologians teach that Romans 10 relates only to salvation, which means they have to ignore the full meaning of the word in the original Greek. *Sozo* means total and comprehensive deliverance and wholeness.

Salvation by grace through faith is a great miracle of God. *To be saved from sin and its curse (poverty, sickness, etc.) is the heart of the Word of faith message.* It is regrettable, if not tragic, that entire denominations have turned away from this positive message, claiming it is overemphasized and is not for all Christians.

It would seem to me that it would be far better to be counted among those who are excessive in their interpretation of faith than to be numbered with those who allow themselves to be robbed of one of the greatest truths taught in the Word of God because of what they think is "overemphasis." Most important, I would not want to be among those who deprive others of this hope.

The Apostle Paul plainly taught the same message that is being taught today: The message of faith means confessing with your mouth that which you believe in your heart.

Confirmation of Romans 10:8 is found in Acts 14:7-10. Paul must have been preaching this message of faith, because he once perceived that a crippled man who had never walked had faith to be healed (*sozo*). That man received a miracle of healing through the preaching of the message of faith in Jesus Christ by Paul.

We must admit there is ample evidence of failure to receive answers to prayers all around us. We hear about many Christians, who were godly, confessed the Word, and believed, yet who died in the end. Because of such incidents, many have turned away from the faith message and want nothing more to do with it.

If true Bible doctrines are going to be judged by human experience, all of us are in trouble! We would have to stop preaching salvation because of the multitudes who have heard yet not been saved through the years. And what about those who heard, confessed Jesus and were saved, yet who turned away and went back into sin?

It is not good judgment to "throw the baby out with the bath water" in any area of life. We must not reject true Bible doctrines because of human failure!

We admit there are many failures where people have claimed the promises of God for salvation, sickness, or financial needs. We could examine some possible reasons for these failures.

The two aspects of the faith message, as we can see from Romans 10:8-10, are believing and confessing. You must believe in your heart, which is a decision, and then confess with your mouth, which is an action. Another meaning of the word *confession* in the Greek is "speaking continual thanksgiving to God."

The same word is interpreted correctly in Hebrews 13:15 in *The Amplified Bible* version:

**Through Him therefore let us constantly and at all times offer up to God a sacrifice of praise, which is the fruit of lips that thankfully acknowledge and confess and glorify His name.**
**[Leviticus 7:12; Isaiah 57:19; Hosea 14:2]**

Not only will salvation be difficult to receive, but so will any other promise that is being confessed before God if the one asking is lacking a spirit of gratitude. Was the one who failed to get an answer a thankful, happy, fulfilled Christian who worshipped God daily?

If the believer is a complainer, always negative, with an "on-again, off-again" lifestyle in serving the Lord, he would probably not receive anything from the Lord. If there is some hidden sin in their life, something they refuse to allow the Holy Spirit to deal with, then they have set up a barrier to receiving the blessings of God.

Most important, if they doubt that God is a good God and lack trust in Him, how can they believe He would ever want them to prosper and be in health?

# Be Careful Not To Reject Paul's Teaching

If Paul had quit preaching this wonderful, positive faith message because of failures, and he saw many, we would not have the message of grace and faith for today.

Having been in contact with many Pentecostal men who have turned against the faith message, I am led to believe they have rejected the "faith teacher" because of imbalance *in their opinions*. In doing this, they have rejected the clear teaching of the Apostle Paul and could find themselves in a ditch of opposition to Scripture.

We who preach and teach the message of faith have been subjected recently to many demeaning titles, such as "name-it-and-claim-it teachers," the "gab-and-grab ministers," and "the health-and-wealth crowd." Being interpreted, these names must mean those who use such terminology do not believe that one can believe a promise and speak out his belief or that God wants them to be blessed.

If that is true, then we certainly would have to reject what the Bible says concerning Abraham and Sarah. God promised them a son and when all hope was gone, Abraham kept on hoping and did not waver. (Romans 4:18,19; Hebrews 11:11.) The promise was not fulfilled until he was a hundred years old and Sarah was ninety-nine years old! In the natural, there was *no* hope, yet they claimed and clung to that promise and eventually received their answer.

Many saints in the Old Testament were given promises, chose to embrace the promises, and confessed them in faith.

(Hebrews 11:13,15,17.) The promises of God are not automatic. If they were, everyone would be saved, healthy, wealthy, and wise. The promises must be believed, received, confessed, and acted upon with thanksgiving.

The kind of faith that pleases God is the kind of faith based on Hebrews 11:6: **Believe that God is.** Believe that He exists. Keep going to Him, even if your faith does not seem to be effective. *Use all of the faith you have, and God will never consider you to be in unbelief.*

Even if you have to have major surgery, keep on believing and confessing how big God is — not how big the problem is — and God will bless the surgeon and the medicine. Whatever you do, however, do not stop going to God. Do not stop confessing that He is God and that He is a rewarder of those who diligently seek Him.

> **But without faith it is impossible to please him; for he that cometh to God must believe that he is, and that he is a rewarder of them that diligently seek him.**
> **Hebrews 11:6**

In the past Christians have equated the word *seek* in the Bible with the parable of the lost sheep or of the lost coins. However, as you are not lost, and God certainly is not lost, *seek* must have another meaning in this context. First of all, it is continuous, meaning to never give up. *"Seek" in this context means to search out and demand, to inquire and require.* [*Strong's Concordance,* "Greek Dictionary," #1567, p. 26.]

If we really believe that God is, and that He is a rewarder of those who *seek* Him, if we continually keep coming to Him, boldly asking and inquiring of Him, He has promised to answer and to reward us.

The kind of faith that pleases God is not necessarily the kind that pleases everyone around you. I recall the testimony of a sister in the Lord who had cancer. She believed that she was healed, but the doctors kept pointing out that cancer was still showing up on the x-rays. In the face of this medical "proof," however, she kept on believing God.

Then she began to suffer from what is known in the medical field as a "hot" appendix, which means one that is ready to burst. They said it must be taken out at once. She said she would let them know after she asked God what to do about it. She inquired of the Lord, and He answered, "Let them take it out."

When the doctors made the incision for the appendix, they said, "While we are in here, let's check on the cancer." They looked but could not find it! It was worth the discomfort of the appendectomy to hear the doctors confess that they could not find the cancer! This is a wonderful example of the faith that inquires of God continually and pleases Him.

Never give up! Use all the faith you have and you will not be in unbelief. Keep on going to Him, keep seeking Him, and He will reward you. Christians say they believe God, but they make major decisions without inquiring of Him. If you really do believe He exists, then act on your faith by checking with God before you make decisions.

## Condemnation Is Wrong

*I would that all pastors teach this faith that pleases God. I would like all Christians to know that, even if they have what looks like a failure of faith, there is no condemnation.* If the first line of defense fails, for whatever reason in the natural, draw back to the next line. But do not waver or give up.

Also, people should be taught not to force their faith on someone else. A pastor especially should meet his people at *their* faith level, not expect members of his congregation to operate at his level of faith.

Pastors, please do not allow your teaching to be influenced by your desire to please people. Sheep, as believers are referred to in the Bible, must be corrected at times, or they will not be healthy sheep. Preach the *whole* counsel of God, not just grace. Teach that *hope* is an integral part of the faith that works.

If a pastor feels apologetic every time he uses the word *faith* in his teaching or preaching, perhaps he already has permitted what he considers to be imbalance to push him into a ditch on the other extreme. Any minister should examine carefully the message he is teaching and make some corrections if they are needed.

The ditches of extremism await all who fail to fight the good fight of faith. It is a message of balance without compromise. It is a message we must never fail to preach, because without it, we cannot please God.

Faith in God and in His Word will always produce positive Christians. Being positive about all things that affect you is not just worldly advice. All Christians are to be considered children of Father Abraham, according to the Apostle Paul. (Galatians 3:9.)

Abraham did not consider his age, one hundred years old, as too old to father a child. God gave to him a great promise, and he determined not to allow his age to keep him from obtaining the promise God had given him.

> **[For Abraham, human reason for] hope being gone, hoped on in faith that he should become the father of many nations, as he had been promised, So [numberless] shall your descendants be.**
> **Romans 4:18 AMP**

> **He did not weaken in faith when he considered the [utter] impotence of his own body, which was as good as dead because he was about a hundred years old, or [when he considered] the barrenness of Sarah's (deadened) womb.**
> **Romans 4:19 AMP**

No unbelief or distrust made him waver or
doubtingly question concerning the promise of God,
but he grew strong and was empowered by faith as he
gave praise and glory to God,

Fully satisfied and assured that God was able and
mighty to keep His word and to do what He had
promised.

**Romans 4:20-21 AMP**

Hope plays an equal role with faith in obtaining
promises. **Faith is the substance of things hoped for**
(Hebrews 11:1). Your faith will not work without hope. But
hope must be spoken. It is not merely a mental attitude.

**Let us be constantly holding fast our confession of
the hope, doing so without wavering, for faithful is He
who promised.**

**Hebrews 10:23 Wuest**

The Bible promises that are to be obtained must have a
strong hope along with faith to be received. It is more than
likely that one does not ever lose all faith, for we always
will believe something — even if it is wrong. What we do is
lose hope, which directs our faith toward the promises of
God for our life.

Abraham kept on hoping when all hope was wrong,
i.e., there seemed to be nothing to hope in and all systems
were negative. But because he kept hoping, his faith kept
on working.

Many opponents of the faith message refer to the failure
of so many people to get answers to their prayers, and thus
they refuse to be identified with the message of faith as
taught by the Apostle Paul. Consequently, they end up in a
ditch of unbelief.

It seems to me that most faith teachers with whom I am
acquainted have made some necessary adjustments
through the years as they mature in the Lord. How about

those who oppose this message? Will *they* do likewise or remain as they are — in opposition to faith?

Bible promises give hope. Confessing your hope keeps faith working in you, and it is by your faith that you keep God well pleased with you. Whether or not you get what you want, just keep on believing and hoping. This delights our Heavenly Father and, yes, He wants you to receive.

He *is* a rewarder of those who diligently keep on seeking Him, inquiring of Him, and requiring from Him. Because God has said this, He requires of Himself that He answer those who seek, inquire, and require.

# 4

# Suffering Saints

Is it God's perfect will for saints to suffer in order for Him to teach them a lesson?

Is it God's perfect will for His very own people to be caught and destroyed in a devastating hurricane or earthquake?

Is it God's perfect will for His own children, redeemed by the blood of His Son, to suffer and die as a result of disease or a plague?

These questions have been debated in the Church for years. On the one side, in a deep ditch, are those who say: "Yes, because we learn more through suffering than we do through being blessed."

On the other extreme are those who teach that if you have enough faith you will never have a trial or test, physical or otherwise.

To have both sides presented so we can have a better understanding should encourage us in the knowledge that we can escape or overcome the things Satan plans for us and that we can know and understand God's attitude toward believers.

Those who are in the ditch of believing that it is God's will to have "bad things happen to good people" should re-examine some of the scriptures they use to "prove" their belief. A book by that title became a best seller a couple of years ago. The Jewish rabbi who wrote it was quoted as making this remark about its popularity: "The popularity had more to do with logic than theology." [*San Diego Tribune*, 1/23/93.]

However, as this book on the subject of ditches will be read primarily by Christians who have been taught by Christians, we will not address the subject from a secular viewpoint. Unbelievers have always viewed the subject much as the residents of Melita did when the poisonous snake bit Paul on their island. (Acts 1:1-11.)

> **And when the barbarians saw the venomous beast** (viper) **hang on his hand** (biting him), **they said among themselves, No doubt this man is a murderer, whom, though he hath escaped the sea, yet vengeance suffereth not to live.**
>
> **Acts 28:4**

When anything catastrophic happens, the world immediately attributes the tragedy to God. Storms and earthquakes are termed "acts of God" by insurance companies. Unfortunately, many Christians have adopted the same attitude.

I recall a Pentecostal leader remarking publicly, when prayer was requested for a woman suffering with cancer, "Rather than praying for her healing, let us thank God for the lessons she will learn through her suffering."

I was shocked to think that the "theology of suffering" had so much influence on Pentecostal believers. When that lady soon passed away, I thought, "Well, she didn't live long enough to be able to practice all she was supposed to have learned!"

Inasmuch as the Apostle Paul's thorn in the flesh seems to have become everyone's prime example of "saints who suffer," I will approach our study from this event in his life.

# Paul's Thorn

**And lest I should be exalted above measure through the abundance of the revelations, there was given to me a thorn in the flesh, the messenger of Satan to buffet me, lest I should be exalted above measure.**

**2 Corinthians 12:7**

People use Paul's "thorn" as an example of physical suffering, comparing it to a sickness or disease which they are enduring. In reality, they could only accurately compare themselves to Paul if they had his revelations!

Paul's "thorn in the flesh" was a "messenger of Satan." A *messenger* in Scripture is an angelic being, demon, or a human being who brings a message. In this case, the messenger was assigned by Satan to hinder Paul's ministry and was most likely a demon. Even today, when we speak of being harrassed by a "thorn in the flesh," it is always a *person or being* of whom we speak, not a *disease.*

Paul's prayer to the Lord was to "let the thorn depart," not to "heal" him. This does not by any stretch of the imagination refer to bad eyes, cancer, or any other type of illness. He had not received a sickness from God to keep him humble; what he resisted was a "special messenger from Satan."

What is even more important, however, is how the Lord answered Paul when he asked Him to take the thorn away, and how Paul reacted to His answer:

**And he said unto me, My grace is sufficient for thee: for my strength is made perfect in weakness. Most gladly therefore will I rather glory in my infirmities, that the power of Christ may rest upon me.**

**Therefore I take pleasure in infirmities, in reproaches, in necessities, in persecutions, in distresses for Christ's sake; for when I am weak, then am I strong.**

**2 Corinthians 12:9,10**

43

# What Are Infirmities?

The Greek word for *infirmities* is translated as "weaknesses" by a number of Bible translators. [Moffatt, Phillips, Weymouth, and Knox; *Twenty-Six Translations.*] Perhaps Knox states it best:

> I am well content with these humiliations of mine, with the insults, the hardships, the persecutions, the times of difficulty I undergo for Christ; when I am weakest then I am the strongest of all. [*Twenty-Six Translations.*]

A physically sick, tormented man could not have made this statement. The trials he endured took great physical strength. In 2 Corinthians 11:23-33, Paul described his infirmities (weaknesses) in great detail: beaten five times, in prison, shipwrecked, in hunger and thirst, many fasts, and constant persecution. None of those listed were sicknesses or diseases.

How could a physically ill and weak man *glory* in those infirmities? He could not have. Paul "gloried" in being "persecuted for Jesus' sake" because he believed Jesus, to whom he had dedicated his life, was glorified through his own weaknesses and incredible obstacles.

For those who have been taught that all sickness and trials are chastisement from God, remember that Paul's "thorn" was not something that would hinder him from traveling, preaching, healing the sick, overcoming persecution and stonings, and being left for dead. It was a "buffeting," not a disability.

Also, Paul did *not* accept the "thorn" *without first praying that it would depart from him.* He persevered in prayer at least three times until he got an answer from the Lord.

Paul did not accept the thorn until he had prayed long enough to find out what really was happening. He did not automatically believe it was from God, and he would not accept anything from Satan until he got an answer from God.

*Paul did not need humbling.* He only needed to be kept from falling because of the abundance of revelation he had received. It was "lest he be exalted above measure" and had nothing to do with physical healing. One who believes that sickness is able to teach them more than Jesus can simply is believing that sickness is a better mentor than the Holy Spirit.

Paul said, "I take pleasure in these weaknesses," because he suffered them at the hands of men for *the sake of the Gospel,* not from God trying to teach him a lesson. When he was weak in those distresses, through Christ, he was so spiritually strong that they could not even kill him! Paul did not die until his work was finished on earth.

One can now better understand what Paul meant when he said:

> **For we would not, brethren, have you ignorant of our trouble which came to us in Asia, that we were pressed out of measure, above strength, insomuch that we despaired even of life:**
>
> **But we had the sentence of death in ourselves, that we should not trust in ourselves, but in God which raiseth the dead:**
>
> **Who delivered us from so great a death, and doth deliver: in whom we trust that he will yet deliver us.**
> **2 Corinthians 1:8-10**

# Suffering Is Not Witnessing

There are also those who believe that God gave them losses or physical sickness to be a better witness for Jesus. They believe, because of the way in which they were taught, that they are suffering for God and by testifying of this suffering they are being good witnesses.

However, there is a lack of logic in that belief, because if they *really* thought it was of God, they would not pray to be healed, take any medicine, or even go to the doctor. If God is sending an illness, it would be wrong to try to shortcut the "lessons" in any way! Seeking to escape from the predicament of sickness would be seeking to get out of God's will.

# Job

Concerning this subject of suffering, there has been more misunderstanding about the book of Job than even about Paul's thorn in the flesh. Many writers refer to the sufferings of this great man in their books, and many preachers refer to him in their sermons, as an example of God's dealings with men.

By far the most references to Job teach that as he suffered so are we to suffer. What they fail to mention is that Job was wonderfully delivered out of all his troubles and richly blessed!

First, we must never use ourselves as an example of Job's sufferings unless we, like Job, are declared to be **perfect and upright, and one that feared God, and eschewed** (hated) **evil** (Job 1:8). Job was in the category of great men of his day, and if there has been another like him, the Bible does not allude to it.

If Job was "perfect" before all of the trials and tribulations hit him — declared to be so by the Almighty God in the presence of heavenly witnesses — how can we use his example to say perfection is *attained* by suffering?

It was not what Job would learn through his trials (and he did learn according to Job 42:1-6). In fact, it wasn't anything he knew or had done that made him perfect. What made him perfect to God was the attitude of his heart. No matter what he faced, Job loved, reverenced, and trusted

God. Why did God call him perfect and upright? Because he "feared God and hated evil." This is an attitude, not an action, and not knowledge. Job made mistakes like any of us, and God even rebuked him in chapter 38, but his attitude of reverence toward God never changed.

If Job was perfect in God's sight, why did he suffer so much? I believe the answer is found in God's simple statement to Satan in Job 1:12, **Behold, all that he** (Job) **hath is in thy power; only upon himself put not forth thine hand.**

As the god of this world, Satan had legal authority over Job, but Job did not know it. In Job 38:2, God said to him:

**Who is this that darkeneth counsel by words without knowledge?**

Those who darken counsel by words without knowledge are those who teach that God causes people to suffer poverty, illnesses, and premature death or that He turns His head as Satan attacks. Even in Job's case, God prevented Satan from touching him personally.

God rebuked Job for daring to open his mouth and speak when he did not understand what was going on or what he was talking about. It is a travesty for pastors and teachers to use the statement of Job that **the Lord gives and the Lord takes away** (Job 1:21) to mean that God was the cause of Job's losing his children and possessions. It was *Satan,* and not God, who took Job's children, health, and possessions.

Placing blame on God for your misfortune impinges on His character. *God is a good God.* Goodness and love are His nature. He is the One on your side! Blame the one who truly brings disease, heartache, and death — Satan. The Apostle John wrote:

**The thief comes only in order that he may steal and may kill and may destroy. I (Jesus) came that they may**

have and enjoy life, and have it in abundance — to the
full, till it overflows.

John 10:10 AMP

# Chastising Is Training, Not Abuse

For whom the Lord loveth he chasteneth, and
scourgeth every son whom he receiveth.

If ye endure chastening, God dealeth with you as
with sons; for what son is he whom the father
chasteneth not?

But if ye be without chastisement, whereof all are
partakers, then are ye bastards, and not sons.

Furthermore we have had fathers of our flesh
which corrected us, and we gave them reverence: shall
we not much rather be in subjection unto the Father of
spirits, and live?

Hebrews 12:6-9

As parents, we must correct our children if they
misbehave. When this is done properly, which means
according to the Bible, it is done with wisdom and love.
(Ephesians 6:4; Colossians 3:21.) God, as our Father, also
has promised to chasten us if we need it.

Would we, as loving parents, chastise our children by
placing diseases on them or causing bodily harm to them?
Then why should we think God would parent us that way?

When parents beat children severely, break their bones,
and leave them with scars, it is called "child abuse." In such
cases the authorities will step in and take children away
from their parents. Yet we accuse God of doing things for
which earthly courts would take away our children! And
we call that the chastening of the Lord.

The Greek word translated *chastisement* is *paideuo*,
which means "to bring up a child, to educate...In a religious
sense, to chastise for the purpose of educating someone to
conform to divine truth." [*The Complete Word Study
Dictionary: New Testament*, by Spiros Zodhiates, #3811.]

God receives us as His children when we are born again, and He teaches and chastens us *by His Word*. In Ephesians 5:25-27, we are told that Jesus is perfecting His bride, the body of Christ, by **the washing of water by the word**.

If you think being chastised by God's Word is never painful, think again! This is the trial of your faith!

The trial of your faith is learning to give tithes and offerings to the Lord with a cheerful heart of thanksgiving.

The trial of your faith is hearing an interpretation of Scripture you've never heard before and, instead of running into a ditch with it, you sit down and study the issue out until you get a balanced perspective.

The trial of your faith is being stretched and tried in order to have a strong marriage and family in an evil world.

The trial of your faith is having to work in an ungodly atmosphere and not be influenced or discouraged, neither giving in to temptations.

The trial of your faith is when you refuse to accept sickness and disease by standing on 1 Peter 2:24 for your health and healing.

In general, living in this world triumphantly as a Christian while being surrounded by evil and ungodliness is the ultimate trial of your faith and source of suffering.

It sounds somewhat humorous, but the New Testament makes it clear that Christians suffer for two reasons: they are in the will of God or out of the will of God.

> **For what glory is it, if, when ye be buffeted for your faults, ye shall take it patiently? but if, when ye do well, and suffer for it, ye take it patiently, this is acceptable with God.**
>
> **1 Peter 2:20**
>
> **Let none of you suffer as a murderer, or as a thief, or as an evildoer, or as a busybody in other men's matters.**

> **Yet if any man suffer as a Christian, let him not be ashamed; but let him glorify God on this behalf.**
> **1 Peter 4:15,16**

Whether we suffer because we "do well" or suffer because we allow our "faults" to overtake us, God is still not the perpetrator of our sufferings!

If you will take the time to look up all of the references in the New Testament concerning suffering, you will note that most of the time we suffer due to persecution because we are living godly lives for the Lord.

> **In this you greatly rejoice, though now for a little while, if need be, you have been grieved by various trials,**
>
> **that the genuineness of your faith, being much more precious than the gold that perishes, though it is tested by fire, may be found to praise, honor, and glory at the revelation of Jesus Christ,**
>
> **whom having not seen you love. Though now you do not see Him, yet believing, you rejoice with joy inexpressible and full of glory.**
> **1 Peter 1:6-8 NKJV**

With this in mind, I think of our oldest son, Dr. Roy Hicks Jr., who loved God and served Him joyfully. This chapter was written only weeks before he went to be with the Lord when the small plane he was piloting crashed into a mountainside during bad weather.

Losing a loved one in this manner is like suffering the severe jolting of a severe earthquake. It is unpredictable and the aftershocks keep coming. But we have, through the prayers and support of many saints, been able to prove and "live out" what Peter taught. When sorrow and grief would rise up and try to defeat us , we have learned to give strong praise to God.

We did not *lose* a son. He has just gone on before us to that wondrous place called Heaven. It is where we — all who have made Jesus Lord of their lives — will soon go and live together with all saints for all eternity.

Margaret and I strongly encourage all who have had to experience sore trials of faith to exercise themselves in strong praise to God. Your faith and trust in Him and His Word, expressed in praise and worship to Him even through terrible pain and suffering, will prove His faithfulness and His love.

# Do We Learn From Suffering?

If suffering itself caused people to be healthy, wealthy, and wise, everyone in the world would be just that. It is not suffering that causes us to become better, but *what we learn from God* through the suffering. And we must always remember that whatever suffering comes our way, **Greater is he who is in you than he who is in the world** (1 John 4:4).

Even if we wilfully sin and backslide like the prodigal son, if we will repent and come back to the Lord with all our heart and surrender our life to Him, He will deliver us out of the mess we have gotten ourselves into and teach us how to avoid falling into the pit again. Nothing in life — whether a blessing or a trial from the devil — is wasted if we allow the Holy Spirit and the Word of God to conform us to the image of Jesus through it.

> **And we know that all things work together for good to them that love God, to them who are the called according to his purpose.**
> **For whom he did foreknow, he also did predestinate to be conformed to the image of his Son, that he might be the firstborn of many brethren.**
> **Romans 8:28,29**

This is why Paul could glory in his sufferings: through each trial, he allowed God to conform him more and more into the image of Jesus. In doing this, he drew closer and closer to his precious Lord and Savior and reached a point of contentment.

> Not that I speak in respect of want: for I have learned, in whatsoever state I am, therewith to be content.
>
> I know both how to be abased, and I know how to abound: every where and in all things I am instructed both to be full and to be hungry, both to abound and to suffer need.
>
> I can do all things through Christ which strengtheneth me.
>
> Philippians 4:11-13

# 5

# Intercession

There is a great need in the Church today for understanding the significance of intercession and its importance to us. In the past decade, there was a clarion call for intercessory prayer in the Body of Christ at large. Saints enrolled in great numbers and formed intercessory prayer groups wherever believers were to be found. It seemed, at last, we were not at a spiritual stalemate, but moving into the battle, the "good fight of faith." (1 Timothy 6:12.)

We had been in a ditch of "little or no" intercessory prayer and needed to get out of it. But we did not need to bound out of that ditch and cross the middle into a ditch that might be even worse!

In the past few years, we have seen some excesses and error in the practice and teaching on intercession. Before we look at these, however, let us first examine what the Bible says intercession is.

> First of all, then, I admonish and urge that petitions, prayers, intercessions, and thanksgivings be offered on behalf of all men.
>
> For kings and all who are in positions of authority or high responsibility, that [outwardly] we may pass a quiet and undisturbed life [and inwardly] a peaceable one in all godliness and reverence and seriousness in every way.
>
> For such [praying] is good and right, and [it is] pleasing and acceptable to God our Savior,

Who wishes all men to be saved and increasingly to perceive and recognize and discern and know precisely and correctly the [divine] truth.

*1 Timothy 2:1-4 AMP*

The Greek word for intercessions is *enteuxis,* which means "A falling in with, meeting with, coming together, intercession, prayer, address to God for oneself or others, prayer according to God's will." [Spiros Zodhiates, *The Complete Word Study Dictionary, New Testament*, #1783.]

The picture this Greek word paints for us is first of all an *intimacy with God.* To intercede, we must "fall in with, meet with, and come together with" God. Second, it denotes addressing God for ourselves and for others in line with God's will, which is always contained in *His Word.* Third, the *purpose* for intercession is that doors of utterance for the Gospel may be opened to all mankind, which is God's will.

The passage of Scripture we have just read from First Timothy tells us that we are to pray and intercede for all men and for those in authority. Why? So we can lead a life of peace inwardly and be able to carry out God's will outwardly, bringing the truth to all men. Intercession brings peace to our inner man and changes circumstances to allow us to continue preaching the Gospel and teaching the Word of God in our social and public life.

Paul was making a distinct call to all saints everywhere and in every age to be in prayer, interceding daily. Intercession can be done privately in our prayer closet, or a group of believers can gather together and pray, even all night. Such praying is good, right, and pleasing to God.

What then are the ditches that believers have fallen into in what seems so clear a mandate from God to carry out? If we pray individually and in groups for all men and those in authority according to God's Word, that the Gospel may come to unbelievers and truth will increase in the lives of believers, where does error enter in?

# Intercession Is For Every Believer

One of the teachings that has arisen in recent years is that intercessory prayer is a special ministry gift in the Body of Christ. I have not been able to find this in Scripture. What we do read in verse after verse is that *all* believers are called by God to intercede.

We are not to think of intercession as a gift bestowed upon a few or even upon certain local churches. Intercession is a calling, a ministry, that all Christians should be carrying out.

Jesus told us that we were to be salt and light. (Matt. 5:13-16.) Salt preserves and adds flavor; light dispels darkness. We retain our savor or saltiness by interceding for all men and those in authority, and the light of God's Word by which we live and that we preach and teach eradicates the darkness, allowing people to receive Jesus and grow in the knowledge of Him.

Intercession is a mandate for all Christians!

# Pulling Down Strongholds

Paul's admonition to Timothy to pray and intercede for those who were in authority had a two-fold purpose, expressed in 1 Timothy 2:4:

**Who will have all men to be saved, and to come into the knowledge of the truth.**

Effective praying will be instrumental in getting people saved and in instructing them in the Word of God. When Paul would enter a city to preach the Gospel, he always encountered the same problem: religion.

The pagan religions and the religious Jews who refused Jesus as the Messiah would try to keep the Gospel from being received through witchcraft, deception, and physical persecution. (See Acts 16:19-24, 17:4-13). Then, after people were saved, the Jews who had been saved would try to get the new converts to deny the grace of God and live by the law. That is why the epistles of Paul are filled with the New Testament revelation of grace versus the law. (See Romans 8:1,2.)

In 2 Corinthians 10:1-6, Paul answers a group of religious Jews who are trying to discredit him by addressing the issue of pulling down strongholds.

> **For though we walk in the flesh, we do not war after the flesh:**
>
> **(For the weapons of our warfare are not carnal, but mighty through God to the pulling down of strong holds;)**
>
> **Casting down imaginations, and every high thing that exalteth itself against the knowledge of God, and bringing into captivity every thought to the obedience of Christ.**
>
> **2 Corinthians 10:2-5**

These verses have been perceived to mean the pulling down of Satan's kingdom over the earth, that believers can actually dethrone the demon powers over a city and "take that city for God." This false teaching, taken to the extreme, has many Christians praying and doing unscriptural things.

The misunderstanding has come with the definition of "strong holds." This is the Greek word *ochuromatos*, which means "A stronghold, fortification, fortress. Used metaphorically of any strong points or arguments in which one trusts." [Spiros Zodhiates, *The Complete Word Study Dictionary, New Testament*, #3794.] Here is Kenneth Wuest's translation of the same verses:

> **For, though we are ordering our behavior in the sphere of human experience, not in accordance with mere human considerations are we waging warfare [against evil], for the weapons of our warfare are not human but mighty in God's sight, resulting in the demolition of fortresses, demolishing reasonings and**

**every haughty mental elevation which lifts itself up against the experiential knowledge [which we believers have] of God, and leading captive every thought into the obedience to the Christ.**

A stronghold is not a demon power, but a system of thought which holds a person's mind captive and hinders them from receiving Jesus Christ as Lord and Savior. The strongholds Paul was tearing down were religious systems of thought. The **imaginations, and every high thing that exalteth itself against the knowledge of God** were the religious thoughts that were blinding the minds of the unbelieving.

However, you cannot say that demon powers are not involved here, because the Bible makes it clear in many verses of Scripture that demons are behind false religions and false teaching among Christians.

**But if our gospel is hid, it is hid to them that are lost:**

**In whom the god of this world hath blinded the minds of them which believe not, lest the light of the glorious gospel of Christ, who is the image of God, should shine unto them.**

2 Corinthians 4:3,4

**Now the Spirit speaketh expressly, that in the latter times some shall depart from the faith, giving heed to seducing spirits, and doctrines of devils.**

1 Timothy 4:1

The context of 2 Corinthians 10:2-5 is that the religious Jews in the church at Corinth were accusing Paul of walking according to natural thinking and not spiritual thinking. They were not saying that Paul was immoral, but that he was teaching false doctrine.

Paul answered them in that passage by saying that, although he did walk and live in the flesh as a man, he did not make warfare by human thinking. He said that his weapons were not carnal, but by God's power he was pulling down strongholds of religious thought. And how do you pull down strongholds of religious thought?

First you intercede by praying for all men to be saved and for favor with those in authority so that the Gospel can be preached and the Word of God taught. At the same time, in the name of Jesus you take authority over all the demon powers who are blinding the minds of those who do not believe (and this includes believers who are in error).

This accomplished, then the Word of God will be preached and taught. Ultimately, it is the Word of God, anointed by the power of the Holy Spirit, which will expose the foolishness of religious thought and cause people to be saved, healed, delivered, and set free.

We cannot get rid of Satan and his demonic powers, but we have been given authority by Jesus, as head of the Church, to bind them from operating in the affairs of men so that God has an entrance into those same affairs. Jesus said:

> **For the Son of man is as a man taking a far journey, who left his house, and gave authority to his servants, and to every man his work, and commanded the porter to watch.**
>
> **Mark 13:34**

Jesus then gave us a picture of how our authority operates in Mark 16:15-18:

> **And he said unto them, Go ye into all the world, and preach the gospel to every creature.**
>
> **He that believeth and is baptized shall be saved; but he that believeth not shall be damned.**
>
> **And these signs shall follow them that believe; In my name shall they cast out devils; they shall speak with new tongues;**
>
> **They shall take up serpents; and if they drink any deadly thing, it shall not hurt them; they shall lay hands on the sick, and they shall recover.**

# Taking Authority

God has the sovereign power to do anything He pleases, but when He created the planet and man, He gave man the authority to rule the earth. (Genesis 1:28.) He must honor His Word even though Adam rejected God and made Satan his new spiritual head, thus making Satan the spiritual head of earth. Jesus Himself called Satan "the prince of this world" (John 14:30), and Paul called him the "god (ruler) of this world" (2 Corinthians 4:4).

The turning point for believers came when Jesus destroyed the works of Satan on the cross (Colossians 2:14; 1 John 3:8) and gained authority over Satan. When He returned to heaven, He delegated that authority to believers on earth. (Matthew 28:18-20; Mark 13:34, 16:15-18.) By the guidelines which He Himself set in the beginning, God can only intervene in man's affairs as the Gospel goes forth in power. That happens through intercession of the saints.

As the Church "occupies" the earth until Jesus returns, we are taking back territory from Satan, who *is* a defeated foe. The Gospel can penetrate, with Holy-Spirit conviction, the hearts of men who have been blinded by Satan.

When missionaries arrived in Argentina many years ago, they were prohibited by law from witnessing or "proselytizing." It was impossible for them to rent a building for church services or even to run an advertisement in the newspaper concerning their meetings.

The missionaries and a few converts began a vigil of prayer that lasted for months. This prayer was not to "pull down Satan" or the ruling powers of Argentina. This fervent, effective praying was to take authority over those ruling powers so that God could give the missionaries favor with the authorities and the people. Then the Gospel could be preached and the Word of God taught to the new converts

Through intercession, demon powers were bound and the missionary evangelist sent there by God found favor with the Perons, who were the dictators at the time. Permits were obtained for meetings to be held in a soccer stadium, and a great revival ensued with miracles, deliverance, and salvation, which continues to this day.

This is also what happened when the walls of Communism began to crumble. Christians outside and behind the Iron Curtain became involved in intercession for the former Soviet Union, and God began to work. Eventually, in His timing, the Berlin Wall came down and for a time the Gospel can be preached in the U.S.S.R.

As intercessors, we will be infinitely more effective if we understand we are not pulling down Satan's kingdom, but binding the demon spirits to give God an avenue through which He can reveal Himself to unbelievers and communicate clearly with believers.

## The Objective is the Truth

The ditches that believers are falling into regarding intercession are too numerous to name, but they all have their root in misunderstanding the manner and purpose of intercession stated in the Scriptures we have just discussed.

Some believers hold great intercessory meetings to take their city for God. They will pray and pray, but when they are finished praying, no one goes out to preach and teach God's Word. Their objective has become prayer, not the purpose of prayer, which is to *accomplish* the Great Commission: to get people saved, healed, and delivered.

Sad to say, many of these well-meaning believers are so intent on pulling down demonic powers that they become obsessed with Satan's kingdom and forget to seek God's kingdom. Ultimately, they are powerless to fight the real strongholds of religious thought which confront them, because they don't have enough knowledge of the Word of God.

# Spiritual Warfare

**For we wrestle not against flesh and blood, but against principalities, against powers, against the rulers of the darkness of this world, against spiritual wickedness in high places.**

**Wherefore take unto you the whole armour of God, that ye may be able to withstand in the evil day, and having done all, to stand.**

**Ephesians 6:12,13**

The Greek word for wrestle is *pale,* and the literal meaning is to shake or vibrate. This word describes two individuals in physical conflict, stuggling in hand-to-hand combat. [Spiros Zodhiates, *The Complete Word Study Dictionary, New Testament,* #3823.]

We are to enter into hand-to-hand combat with the demon rulers of this world system, and verse 12 describes a hierarchy of them. However, the name and authority of Jesus is greater than Satan himself, so any demon under him must also be subject to us in Jesus' name.

Verse 13 describes *how* we are to wrestle with these principalities and powers: by putting on the whole armor of God. This was what Paul was referring to when he said that the weapons of his warfare were **mighty through God.** James 4:7 tells us the order of things in spiritual warfare:

**Submit yourselves therefore to God. Resist the devil, and he will flee from you.**

The Greek word for "Resist" is the same word used in Ephesians 6:13 for "withstand." It literally means "to stand against and resist in word or deed." [Spiros Zodhiates, *The Complete Word Study Dictionary, New Testament,* #436.]

We have many Christians who are praying against and doing things they believe are stopping the devil without first submitting themselves to God. Therefore, they do not know what they are doing or why they are doing it. Instruction for effective praying is taught in Romans 8:26,27. True intercession for saints must be by the Holy Spirit, for only the Holy Spirit knows what is really going on in the spirit realm and in the natural realm.

Along this line of thinking, let us take a look at "warring tongues." This is a recent practice of Christians who purposely pray in tongues loudly and militantly with a specific objective in mind (such as binding the principalities and powers over a city). Essentially, they are trying to instruct the Holy Spirit *how and where* to do His work. To do so could grieve Him and even might be a sin against Him.

We are always to submit ourselves to the leading of the Holy Spirit first, praying according to the Word of God in the language we speak, and in tongues when we do not know how to pray. Without surrendering ourselves to His guidance, we are praying and interceding according to our own flesh and carnal thinking.

We can only wrestle with the demon powers involved in a situation and accomplish God's will in the matter when we have submitted our hearts and minds to the Holy Spirit and allowed Him to "run the show." Then we are interceding in the power and wisdom of God and not our own. Again, we are giving God an entrance to move in the affairs of men.

Firmly resist being drawn into any involvement in prayer, intercessory or otherwise, where the perimeters are not clear from Scripture, and you will avoid the ditches into which many have fallen.

Always remember that we do not have the power to change a man's will who wishes to serve Satan. The only way this can be accomplished is for that man to receive Jesus Christ as his Lord and Savior. However, by our prayers and binding Satan, we give the Holy Spirit a legal right to bring heavy conviction upon them. And, if they do not receive Jesus, our prayers give God the legal right to keep them from hindering His work in our lives and in the earth.

This chapter is written to encourage all believers to be *continuously* praying and interceding according to the Word of God. All Christians are intercessors, not just a few.

If there ever was a time in our nation's history that a clarion call to prayer was needed, it is now! The continuation of freedom and finances to spread our wonderful Gospel depends upon our earnest supplications and prayers being made in intercession without ceasing.

# 6

# Divorce and Remarriage

When one discusses imbalance and ditches, the subject of divorce and remarriage must certainly be considered very carefully. Perhaps one will find no other subject that will produce a wider margin of difference. The extremes range from "Absolutely not, under no circumstances!" to "Yes, for even the slightest of differences."

It is ironic that in denominations and churches where the Bible is considered the inerrant Word of God, misunderstanding abounds. Many believe that divorce and remarriage are unacceptable for any reason. Some believe divorce is acceptable only when one spouse commits adultery, but most treat divorce and remarriage like they are unpardonable sins!

Only those churches who are taught the whole council of God on this subject are set free from the bondage of legalism that seems to surround this subject and forever cause strife and division in the church, not to mention great misunderstanding and heartache among belivers who are touched by divorce and remarriage.

Legalism always looks to the law for spirituality and places great emphasis on certain Old Testament guidelines:

• In Leviticus 21:14, we are told that a high priest could not marry either a widow *or* a divorced woman.

• In Leviticus 22:13, it is written that if a daughter divorced or became a widow, she could return to her father's house (the high priest's house) and eat from the "holy" food — if she remained single.

• These laws set a very high standard for the high priest and his family. However, there was quite a different law set for "lay people" in Deuteronomy 24:1,2. They were allowed to divorce and remarry.

In Matthew 19:3-9, the Pharisees asked Jesus about the question of divorce relative to the Old Testament verses above. Their intent was to trap Him and justify their own hypocrisy. At that time, they divorced and remarried for the most ludicrous reasons.

Jesus answered them with what *Elohim* had in mind when man was created and given a "helpmeet": A man and a woman are to be married, become one flesh, and not return to their parents. What God has joined together, let no man separate. He was referring to Genesis 2:24,25.

The Pharisees thought they had caught Jesus in a trap, so they asked, "Why, then, did Moses grant our fathers the privilege of divorcing their wives?"

Jesus answered, "Because of the hardness of their hearts."

If you look up *hardness* in *Strong's Concordance* , you will find that the Greek word not only means "hardness of heart" but "destitution of (spiritual) perception in your heart." (*Strong's Concordance*, #4641, p. 65.]

Jesus then gave the interpretation of the meaning of Moses' words in Deuteronomy 24:1: You can only put her away because of uncleanness (sexual sins) she has committed. He did not *change* what Moses said about the woman being free to remarry. (See Deuteronomy 24:2.)

Actually, Jesus was addressing the *man* as the one not having liberty to remarry—if he put his wife away for any other reason than sexual impurity. [Note: the later Greek manuscripts omit the last part of Matthew 19:9, which says that anyone who marries a woman who has been divorced commits adultery.]

# What Jesus Was Really Saying

The disciples, hearing what Jesus said to the Pharisees, reasoned among themselves that, if Moses' words referred to a man not being free to divorce and remarry, then perhaps it would be better to stay single! (Matthew 19:10.)

The fact that a couple becomes *one in marriage* seemed to put heavy accountability on the man for the success of the marriage, because the Jewish culture looked on the man as of greater significance than the woman.

In the light of this responsibility, the disciples thought perhaps it would be better not to marry at all. In that day, men were easily divorcing their wives and remarrying for any and all reasons. The wives, however, were usually not free to remarry. Jesus was telling them that they could not continue to do this and remain right with God.

The disciples never did seem to understand the complex answer to the Pharisees' question, nor have believers been able to agree on what Jesus really meant since that time. But it is clear that He allowed divorce for hardness of heart and for sexual sin, and He did not contradict Moses' statement that it was acceptable to remarry after divorce.

# New Testament Teachings on Divorce and Remarriage

I will attempt to give what I believe to be a paraphrase of what the New Covenant has to say on this difficult and complex question. It will, no doubt, still not completely satisfy everyone who reads this book. But bear with me, as we carefully work our way through some of the scriptures.

New Testament believers do not function under the Old Testament law, because it was impossible to keep. If you broke one, you were guilty of breaking them all. (Romans 7:2-5.) Christ is the end of the law. (Romans 10:4.) It is the blood of Jesus, not of animals, whereby we are made righteous.

That era of the law being over, we are now under a new commandment and law: the law of love. Romans 13:10 tells us that love is the fulfilling of the law. Jesus said:

> **A new commandment I give unto you, That ye love one another; as I have loved you, that ye also love one another.**
>
> **John 13:34**

It is only in keeping the "new" commandment of Jesus that you can honor God's original idea for a man to leave his mother and father and "cleave" unto his wife so that they become one flesh. (Genesis 2:24.)

The most predominant scripture passage dealing with divorce and remarriage in the New Testament epistles is found in 1 Corinthians 7:1-17 and 27-28. Here Paul wrote, "I will speak," meaning that what he was about to say had not been previously recorded nor was it the words of Jesus. Paul certainly was not inferring that the Lord had one opinion and he had another. He simply was giving a further explanation.

Paul affirmed that he spoke by the Spirit of God to the churches, and we know that all Scripture was given by inspiration of God. (2 Timothy 3:16.) Paul referred to some questions the Christians at Corinth must have asked him in a previous letter. In other words, he is not opening this subject on his own, but answering some things they had asked, things we are still asking today.

The following is a paraphrase of his teaching in Corinthians:

A husband or wife should not put an end to a marriage even if the mate is an unbeliever *if* that unsaved mate wants the marriage to work and makes an effort toward that end. (1 Corinthians 7:12,13.) Paul gives great hope that the unbelieving one eventually will get saved if the couple stays together.

This admonition to stay together has a bearing on whether or not the children of this marriage are considered to be holy in the eyes of the Lord. (1 Corinthians 7:14.) Under the Old Covenant, all of the children of heathen were deemed to be unclean by the Jews, and their own children considered to be "holy." Remember in that day, children of heathen parents had been dedicated to heathen gods upon or even before birth. [Clarke's *Commentary*, Vol. 6, p. 223.]

On the other hand, Paul says that if the unbelieving husband or wife leaves, the believing mate is no longer bound to the marriage. The reason given is that the believing mate cannot save the unbelieving mate (1 Corinthians 7:15-16.)]

In verse 27 Paul says that if you are married, don't get a divorce and if you are divorced, don't seek to be married again. This verse, read without verse 28, has caused many Christians to falter in the faith if they were divorced because they have been told they could never remarry if they were divorced. However, in verse 28 Paul goes on to say that *if you do remarry you have not sinned!*

Some people, reading this for the first time, may be shocked, thinking that the Apostle Paul was contradicting the Lord Jesus Christ. This is impossible, if one believes that all Scripture was given by inspiration of God. Paul merely was making a transition from the teachings of the Old Covenant of Law to the New Covenant of grace and love.

I recall a time when a heartbroken wife poured out her grief because her husband had left her for a younger woman and had fathered children by that woman. She understood, by the tradition of her church, that she had to remain single for the rest of her life.

But I pointed out these verses in 1 Corinthians 7 that, according to my understanding, inasmuch as her husband had exhibited that he was no longer pleased to dwell with her by his infidelity, she was free from the bondage of that marriage. And, according to 1 Corinthians 7:28, she would not sin if she did remarry.

All through these verses, Paul stresses the fact that marriage should not be dissolved for any "flippant" reason, but the couple should work out their differences and create a pleasant environment, especially where children are involved. Whether she is pleased to dwell with him and he is pleased to dwell with her is the only criterion that determines whether or not the marriage will continue.

If either spouse is having an extramarital affair, it would seem that he or she is no longer "pleased" to dwell with the other. In this case, the offending one has chosen to conduct himself or herself as the heathen do. Because of this, the Apostle Paul now deems the one faithfully serving the Lord to be free.

Not only do we base this on Jesus' words in Matthew 19:9 and Deuteronomy 24:1, but God himself set the precedent in Jeremiah 3:8, when He divorced Israel because of their spiritual harlotry.

Nevertheless, believers today are ultimately to act according to the law of love, which includes forgiveness and restoration. If the mate who has committed adultery has truly repented, their husband or wife should forgive them and allow God to restore the marriage.

No marriage involving Christians should be hastily dissolved. The souls of the children and the backslidden one could be jeopardized if there is a divorce. Instead, a period of separation sometimes will give each one time to reconsider and may lead to reconciliation.

Paul's teaching does not free one to leave his or her mate merely because there is a desire to do so. He makes it very clear that the husband is to love his wife as Christ loves the Church, and the wife should obey her husband. (See Ephesians 5:22-33.) The marriage should work with much give and take, adjusting, and repairing.

If you are married you know what is meant here. We, as New Testament Christians, are to work hard at making our marriages successful. New Testament love and the grace of God carry an awesome responsbility to live a Christ-like life. In counseling, I always endeavor to point out the Bible's admonition, **the two shall become one flesh**, and every possible effort should be made to keep from breaking that bond.

However, if that bond has been broken, divorce and possibly remarriage has taken place, we are to treat these believers with the same love and respect we would those who are virgins! This is the law of love.

## Confusion Over Divorce and Remarriage Wreaks Havoc

Many denominations that treat divorce as an unpardonable sin have wrought much havoc among their members. These ministers call for forgiveness if someone committed adultery, theft, or even murder. When a sinner is invited to receive Christ, they inform him that Christ alone can forgive his sin, and that by receiving Him, all sins of the past are not only forgiven but put in the sea of God's forgetfulness.

Those who have a wonderful salvation experience and rejoice that their past is forgiven have a rude awakening if they decide to go to Bible school and are divorced. In those denominations and churches, it does not matter that they are saved and feel the call of God on their life, they are not welcome. It is a severe blow to hear that because they have been divorced they are now prohibited from being licensed with that denomination.

It defies reason to think that a man who has led a life of fornication and left fatherless children across the nation, repented, and joined the church can become a minister; on the other hand, if he had married one of the girls and given their child a name, but the marriage ended in divorce, *he would be denied* the opportunity of serving the Lord as a minister.

Does it make sense that a man or woman should be denied the privilege of serving God in ministry because he or she did the right thing? The world looks upon such logic as tremendous hypocrisy, and this kind of legalism turns many unbelievers away from God and the church.

Ultimately, the law of love makes good common sense. Believers know it instinctively in their hearts, because the Spirit of God can only tell them the truth. That is why tremendous confusion reigns in their lives when they are taught traditional religious thinking and legalism instead of what the Bible really says, especially a divorced person.

In their hearts, they know God has cleansed them of the sin of divorce. Or, if they were a victim to divorce—their spouse deserted them—they know they are blameless and free. Yet their spiritual leadership does not allow them to work in the church and other members treat them as though they are guilty because they are divorced.

In their hearts, they also know it is acceptable to remarry, but those in spiritual authority and the members surrounding them tell them they will sin if they remarry, that God can never acknowledge or bless that union. If they do eventually remarry, they are shunned by their church.

This is grievous in light of the law of love we are to live by in the body of Christ. Judgmentalism and legalism grieves the Holy Spirit and causes great devastation to believers, families, churches, and whole denominations.

# Guidelines for New Testament Believers

If you are a Christian and you have been through divorce and/or remarriage, here are some guidelines that may help you.

1. The Bible does not teach that divorce and remarriage are unpardonable sins.

2. The Bible does teach that there is freedom for the innocent party if the spouse backslides and is unfaithful to the marriage vow, *and* if the unfaithful spouse no longer desires to be involved in a Christian marriage.

3. If you were divorced (even more than once), all of that is under the blood when you received Jesus or repented. First John 1:9 cleanses us from all unrighteousness, and that includes divorce.

4. In the light of the above, you are saved and forgiven of your past, and you are free to obey His call on your life.

5. If you are divorced, be much in prayer for direction and take time to heal and become strong in the Lord before considering remarriage. Rushing into another marriage directly after divorce will only bring the problems from the first marriage into the second.

6. Seek to make your marriage, even if it is not your first one, a happy one. Shun all thoughts of ending it.

# The Attitude of the Heart

The most devastating aspect of this issue of divorce and remarriage is the judgmentalism that comes from those who do not know what the Bible really says about it. They look upon those who have been divorced and are now remarried as adulterers, living in sin and forever banished from the blessings of God—even if God is obviously blessing them, their marriage, and any children who come of that marriage! They consider the divorced and/or remarried person as a second-class believer.

A word of warning to those who have taken such a harsh stand against divorce and remarriage that you have caused many believers to be caught in a tangled web of confusion. If you take the law of the Old Testament that Jesus spoke and call those who are remarried after a divorce "adulterers," you had better read Matthew 5:27,28.

If you think you have a "license" to cast a stone, you had better examine your own heart carefully. Any man who ever has *looked* with lust at a woman more than once is considered an adulterer in the New Covenant. Be very careful how you regard people who are divorced!

Most of all, beware of the wiles of the devil. It is his plan to wreak havoc in the life of all believers by casting them into a ditch of guilt where there is little hope of escape. The grace of God is available for all people, no matter what the sin — even divorce. Remember the cleansing blood of Jesus (1 John 1:9). It is His grace and cleansing that inspire us not to sin again and allow us to forgive others their sin.

Consider this: *If the New Testament is the fulfilling of all the Old Testament laws, then to act contrary to the New Testament law of love would be a violation of both the Old and New Testaments.*

The New Testament law of love does not infer that it is an inferior standard of obedience and holiness compared to the Old Testament laws. In the New Testament, the law of love and grace inspires us to keep a standard of holiness. Simply put, our love for God and our love for others gives us the will and strength not to sin!

If a Christian truly loves the Lord, he will not want to sin against the Lord or break His commandments.

If a Christian truly loves his brothers and sisters, he will not want to sin against them.

If two Christians live according to the law of love, they should not divorce.

When we apply the law of love to the issue of divorce and remarriage and then study the New Testament scriptures dealing with it, we see that divorced people who caused their divorce can be forgiven and those who were victims of divorce can forgive and go on with their lives, even remarrying.

We should never encourage divorce or shun the standard of holiness set for us in the Bible, but let us not put believers in bondage when Jesus Christ has set them free!

# 7
# Hero Worship

This chapter contains a closer look at how we perceive people, based on their deeds, performance, and achievements. Its purpose is not to be judgmental, but to examine in the light of the Word of God what is considered appropriate or inappropriate conduct for public figures in the Body of Christ and how they should handle the precious things of God.

A curious thing takes place when people, even people in the religious world, become widely known. They become public property in a sense, and people in every walk of life seem to express opinions about them. We hear comments such as, "I just love him," or "I can't stand him."

A friend of mine was visiting with another friend who made a particularly angry remark about a very well-known evangelist. His moral failure had become a matter of public knowledge. When my friend tried to soften the attitude of his friend toward the fallen evangelist, his friend said, "I know it is wrong, but I still hate him."

Inasmuch as the subject of this book is ditches that are a constant threat to a Christian's spiritual balance, I felt strongly that this subject should be included. As with some of the other subjects, it seems that the middle ground is hard to find. However, we must make a dedicated effort to find it in the interest of our credibility in the world.

The extremes of admiring a public figure to the point of "hero worship " or despising that person judgmentally must be dealt with. One extreme tends toward idolatry and the other toward bitterness and hatred, both which put one's soul in jeopardy.

I do not want to further wound any minister who has fallen, nor do I want to harm in any way the tens of thousands of godly ministers who are serving the Lord to the best of their abilities. But I feel an obligation to write this chapter as a warning to all of us about how easily we can move from the middle of the road without even being aware we have moved!

An example of people moving from love to hate is found in Acts 14:7-19. A man who had been born crippled was marvelously healed through the ministry of the Apostle Paul. The people who witnessed this miracle began to cry, **The gods are come down to us in the likeness of men.** (Acts 14:11.)

As they prepared to worship and sacrifice to Paul and Barnabas, the apostles saw what was happening. They tore their clothes, the symbol of grief and mourning in those days.

> **And saying, Sirs, why do ye these things? We also are men of like passions with you, and preach unto you that ye should turn from these vanities unto the living God, which made heaven, and earth, and the sea, and all things that are therein.**
>
> **Acts 14:15**

Then certain Jews came and persuaded the people to a negative opinion about the apostles, and the people turned on them, stoned Paul, and left him for dead. (Acts 14:19.) The people moved so quickly from love and adulation to hatred and murder that Paul almost lost his life.

It is my hope that the thoughts contained in this chapter will help all who read it to reject wide swings of emotion concerning public figures. I pray that all Christians learn to truly love people, but not be hero worshippers. We need to stay in balance by the truth that there is only one hero to worship, and that is Jesus Christ.

Many times, while serving in an official capacity in my denomination, I had to meet with people and endeavor to help them put their lives back together because their pastors, whom they dearly loved, had fallen into sin.

These situations are devastating to saints, because they are faced with the fact that their leaders are not perfect. They are human just like everybody else.

The Bible offers an excellent way to love and respect leaders without putting them on pedestals. In Luke 17:6, Jesus told the disciples that they could tell a tree to be pulled up by the roots and cast into the sea if they had the faith of a grain of mustard seed. Then, in verses 9 and 10, lest they become self-righteous, He told a parable about a good servant who works in the fields all day, then comes in and fixes supper for the master before he can stop to rest and fix something for himself to eat. The one referred to as a *servant* is likened to all of us who serve the Lord.

Jesus asked this question:

> "Does he thank that servant because he did the things that were commanded him? I think not.
>
> So likewise you, when you have done all those things which are commanded you, say, 'We are unprofitable servants: we have done that which was our duty to do.'"
>
> **Luke 17:9, 10 NKJV**

Jesus is not saying this to be mean! He is making the point that whether we are performing incredible miracles or simply making a meal, we are all merely servants of God.

Something else Jesus said along these lines also should be remembered:

And whoever wishes to be most important and first in rank among you must be the slave of all.

For even the Son of man came not to have service rendered unto Him, but to serve, and to give His life as a ransom for (instead of) many.

**Mark 10:44,45 AMP**

Mutual love and respect between pastors and their flocks and continuing in the scriptures by all will minimize the danger of falling into the ditches of either hero worship or hatred.

# Religious Heroes Are Not New

Famous televangelists and megachurch pastors may appear to be a new phenomenon in Christianity, but actually, religious leaders have been public figures before. What is happening today is a repetition of the past in many ways.

In the Roman Catholic Church, it has not been unusual for popes to be treated as infallible. Indeed, the doctrine of papal infallibility and a pope's misuse of power through the sale of indulgences was the "straw that broke the camel's back" when Martin Luther split with the church in 1517. The pontiff in question was Leo X of the House of Medici, member of a wealthy family of bankers, merchants, and rulers in a couple of small nations that now are included in Italy.

Pope Leo needed vast funds to complete the building of the new St. Peter's Cathedral in Rome. To pay for it, he came up with one of the greatest money-making plans ever devised in the religious realm.

For a considerable offering to the church, one could purchase his deceased relatives' release from Purgatory. This is a place between earth and heaven where Catholics believe everyone goes when they die. If the still-living relatives prayed hard enough, their deceased relative might be released more quickly into heaven.

Money flooded into the church's coffers, and St. Peter's was finished at a very high cost to the Roman Catholic Church, not the least of which was the Protestant Reformation.

Some evangelists sell "indulgences" today, but with greater sophistication and subtlety than did Pope Leo X. Prayer cloths, vials of holy water supposedly from the Jordan River, and various trinkets, along with a promise to spend time in prayer for your personal needs, will be sent if you send them an offering. Does this kind of telemarketing not remind you of the sale of indulgences?

It is not inconceivable that God would give such a strategy to a minister in order to give the believer a tangible point of contact on which to release their faith for a miracle. But for the above-mentioned reason, I admonish them that *God,* rather than their own reasoning or a marketing committee, better have told them to do something along these lines before you do it!

Most televangelists and megachurch pastors retain their integrity and positively affect the lives of millions. These men would be shocked to be called "superstars," yet like it or not, almost every such nationally-known minister or teacher is just that to many Christians. Their lives and actions are watched by millions.

## Living Vicariously

Most of humanity, without Jesus, are losers in life, cut off from the Creator and without purpose. Satan always has devised clever pacifiers for people who lead quiet, desperate lives filled with fear, disappointment, and grief. One such pacifier is found in the output of the entertainment industry.

For a few hours, people can escape from the reality of their dreary lives by watching the "stars" do and say things on television or at the movies that they would give anything to be able to do and say.

"Fans" love it when their favorite stars go from bed to bed and party to party. The more outrageous the stars' behavior, the more they are idolized.

Sometimes newly saved Christians simply exchange the vicarious lives they lived through idolizing movie stars with trying to live through the lives of famous evangelists and teachers. The unfortunate result is Christians who are spiritual cripples.

They do not know the difference between the presence of the Holy Spirit and showmanship, because their own spiritual lives are focused on the ministerial "stars" whom they follow, rather than developing a personal relationship with Jesus.

# Accountability in Leadership

Regarding the ministry, it is important for the Church to understand the deadly effects of the abuse of power. Matthew 19:24 says:

> **And again I say unto you, It is easier for a camel to go through the eye of a needle, than for a rich man to enter into the kingdom of God.**

One of the major reasons for the spiritual downfall of the rich is that money brings power, and as Lord Acton said in 1887, "Power tends to corrupt; absolute power corrupts absolutely." [Bartlett, John. *Familiar Quotations* (Boston: Little, Brown, and Co., 13th Ed., 1955, p. 663.]

When one has this kind of power, he can move from a position of preaching sound doctrine to a position of doctrinal abuse, because Satan will deceive him into thinking his power and position make him immune to rebuke or criticism. The abuse of doctrine can lead to severe results, among which is grieving the Holy Spirit.

If integrity is being compromised repeatedly, but only a little at a time, a leader can convince himself that no one is being hurt. However, the compromise of integrity is a corrosive process, and if it is allowed to continue it will eventually completely isolate him from the reality of his sin. Because he does not abide in the truth, he is deceived. This is what happens to evangelists and pastors who fall.

The adulation of the masses, the attention received from staffs of people who shield famous ministers from the public, and the vast sums of money being rushed from the services back to the hotel suites can serve to bring about corrupted attitudes in those "stars." Such a well-known speaker can be led by these things to believe that he is above the law, both God's and man's.

These leaders are often accountable to no one when caught defrauding people out of millions of dollars or when committing some sexual vice. They simply move to another town and begin a new church or ministry and repeat the past.

The Church, to a large extent, has no established procedure to halt or expose these abuses. As a result, we find our ministers being tried in worldly courts in a media circus, which is a terrible hindrance to the Church's ability to preach the gospel to the lost.

*Christians should not have to learn about the misconduct of spiritual leaders in the tabloids found in supermarkets or on the network evening news.*

As Christians, we must move to a position of accountability in leadership. However, we must do this without the rebounding action that usually accompanies correction, which can result in terrible events like the Inquisition. We do not want to move from one ditch to another.

At this point in time, we seem to have been in a ditch that quotes, **Touch not mine anointed** (1 Chronicles 16:22), when correction is brought to such leaders. We have been through a period when no one would raise a voice to protest what were obvious abuses.

We do not want to protest the abuses to the point where we end up in the ditch of extreme criticism; but it is well to remember that if we are to operate by the Old Testament admonition to "touch not God's anointed," then Martin Luther was wrong when he exposed Pope Leo X on his abuses and unscriptural practices.

The Apostle Paul also would be in the wrong when he severely corrected the Apostle Peter openly for hypocrisy.

> **But when Peter was come to Antioch, I withstood him to the face, because he was to be blamed.**
>
> **But when I saw that they walked not uprightly according to the truth of the gospel, I said unto Peter before them all, If thou, being a Jew, livest after the manner of Gentiles, and not as do the Jews, why compellest thou the Gentiles to live as do the Jews?**
>
> **Galatians 2:11,14**

We should acknowledge the many faithful televangelists and megachurch pastors who serve God out of a committed, surrendered life. At the same time, we must have compassion for the sheep who have been duped out of their life savings and money they could not afford to lose. Their souls have been so wounded they may never heal! May we find a mature and balanced way of holding our ministers accountable in order to prevent this travesty.

# Worship God Only

Let us be careful how we regard those who are in ministry. If we regard them as superhuman and idolize them to the point of hero worship, we have forsaken our first love, Jesus.

And leaders, if your followers, in their immaturity, begin to idolize you as their hero, beware of coming to believe you are above reproach and correction. As soon as you discern they are putting you on a pedestal that only belongs to God, address the issue and set them straight. You are warned of this in Romans 12:3:

> **For I say, through the grace given unto me, to every man that is among you, not to think of himself more highly than he ought to think; but to think soberly, according as God hath dealt to every man the measure of faith.**

In the New Covenant, we have the Holy Spirit dwelling in us. But many Christians are running around the country and the world after their own personal hero, thinking they can only receive from God from them. This is the action of a baby Christian, who will only grow to maturity as they are faithful to their local church and the teaching of God's Word.

> **If ye abide in me, and my words abide in you, ye shall ask what ye will and it shall be done unto you.**
>
> **John 15:7**

Yes, there is a true move of the Holy Spirit when we come together. There are times when a saint being prayed for by a man or woman of God whom they highly respect will receive great miracles. But the Holy Spirit *in us* is the One who works the miracles. (See Acts 3:12,13,16.)

Here is another question for those believers who habitually go from meeting to meeting: "Can the emotional 'high' that I get when I attend these meetings give me any answers to problems that the Word of God cannot give?"

We must determine whether the Holy Spirit is compelling us to seek the counsel and prayer of a leader for what we are in need of or calling us to search His Word and seek the Lord. Perhaps we are to go to a brother or sister in the Lord who will minister to us what God wants us to know or receive.

It is true that many times the apostles laid their hands on people to receive healing, miracles, the baptism of the Holy Spirit, and to send forth ministers. But real maturity in the Lord comes when we worship and look first to God for all the issues of life. He will send us to the right people at the right time, or He will directly give us whatever we need or seek.

# 8

# Praise and Worship

An observation I have made in recent years is that Christians seem to be so mixed up about Old and New Testament worship that they are in neither the Old nor the New! Just what are the differences between Old Testament and New Testament forms of worship?

## God Inhabits His People Today

Under the Old Covenant, God inhabited the praises of Israel. All praise was done with this in mind.

> But thou art holy, O thou that inhabitest the praises of Israel.

> Psalm 22:3

Under the New Covenant, God inhabits *us:*

> Know ye not that ye are the temple of God, and that the Spirit of God dwelleth in you?

> 1 Corinthians 3:16

> What? know ye not that your body is the temple of the Holy Ghost which is in you, which ye have of God, and ye are not your own?

> 1 Corinthians 6:19

It seems that a great majority of choruses written and sung in the last few years deal with Old Covenant truth which was good, but not applicable today. We live under a "better" covenant. (Hebrews 8:6.)

Did Jesus promise to be with Christians whenever they met, waiting as we sang and praised Him for forty-five minutes before He came into our midst? Or do we believe He is there by faith? Do we have to "feel" His presence?

If He truly inhabits us, then the object of praise and worship is not to *feel* His presence so we can have a better church service, but to *honor* His presence through our praise and worship.

Yes, we are to sing praises and worship when we come together, but the motive is *not* to bring the presence of God into our midst. The presence of God is not in a service because we sing and worship. The presence of God is there because *He promised never to leave us.*

Where praise and worship was done at certains times and places in the Old Testament, under the New Covenant praise and worship to our God is a lifestyle. It is to be done in willing obedience and not only on Sundays. The Father is not seeking "Sunday worshippers." He is looking for true worshippers who praise and worship Him continually.

*We are to worship the Lord as a lifestyle.*

**But the hour cometh, and now is, when the true worshippers shall worship the Father in spirit and in truth: for the Father seeketh such to worship him.**
**John 4:23**

Pure worship must be in the Holy Spirit and according to the truth of God's Word. Merely mouthing words that someone else wrote is not sufficient. Praise and worship must come out of your heart and spirit, praising and worshipping Him for Who He is, what He has promised, and what He has done and is doing.

A person who is not born again, who is without the Holy Spirit residing within and therefore has little comprehension of the Word of God, cannot truly worship God. But there is a wonderful "sense of His presence" whenever Christians gather together in spirit and in truth.

# Why Do We Meet?

The true reason for our gathering together is to be in obedience to the Word of God in Hebrews 10:25:

**Not forsaking the assembling of ourselves together, as the manner of some is; but exhorting one another: and so much the more, as ye see the day approaching.**

We gather together to have fellowship, hear the Word of God taught, and provide an atmosphere in which people can get saved.

Music and singing praise and worship will bring an awareness of an intimate relationship with the Lord, but then it is the Word of God that is taught in that atmosphere which causes the saints to grow and mature.

**It is the spirit that quickeneth; the flesh profiteth nothing: the words that I speak unto you, they are spirit, and they are life.**
**John 6:63**

I have often wondered, if one of the motives for worship is to open up the human spirit to receive the engrafted Word of God, which feeds our spirits and builds us up, why do we praise and worship — then receive the offering, have special music, announcements, and so forth *before* the pastor opens the Word?

It seems to me that we have just defeated the reason for worship by separating the time of worship from ministry of the Word. Why do that if praise and worship are to prepare us to receive the Word?

Along these lines, my suggestions to pastors are these:

1. Have the singing of praise to get your congregation settled down and truly aware of why they are in the service. My good friend Dick Mills says this schedule is to "get your people from the parking lot to the throne."

2. After *this* is a good time for offerings, announcements, special music, if any, and any other activities.

3. Then you can have your music team, who have remained on the platform, lead a time of pure worship with and in the Spirit.

4. When you have a witness from the Holy Spirit, immediately step up and give the precious Word to open, receptive hearts. There are pastors who are doing this and experiencing great benefits and growth.

# Pure Worship

Under the New Covenant, we are to become worshippers whose worship is made pure by the Spirit within us and by our obedience in a daily relationship and communion with our Lord. But there are practical considerations which help pastors and their congregations maintain an atmosphere of pure worship to God.

Having been around ministry for five decades, may I humbly suggest to pastors that, if you do have a long time of praise, please allow the people the privilege of either standing or sitting. Also, *and this is important, the pastor is the one who is to be in control of the length of worship time.* He will know when the time for the Word has come or when the time for the gifts of the Spirit has come.

Dancing before the Lord can be a spontaneous expression of *joy* if done decently and in order. But the choreographed routines performed by beautiful, shapely young women clad in sheer costumes over leotards do nothing to enhance the spirituality of a church service. Men who sit in the congregation, perhaps just recently saved, will not be spiritually blessed by the sight. Indeed, they will have to keep their eyes closed if they are to have any semblance of a spiritual mind.

What we must avoid, in whatever forms of worship we use, is taking attention from God or His Word and placing it upon ourselves. By doing this, we could be in grave danger of grieving the Holy Spirit.

# New Testament Practices of Worship

Most of what we believe and practice in the area of worship is based on the fourth chapter of John, which records the incident when Jesus met the sinful woman at the well of Samaria.

When she encountered Jesus, the woman at the well immediately challenged Him as to which was the true place to worship God — in Jerusalem or in Samaria. The answer Jesus gave her essentially was, "Neither one."

The time and the place were not the issue. The issue was *how* we worship. Jesus took worship out of the public forum and placed it in the hearts of individual worshippers.

> **Jesus saith unto her, Woman, believe me, the hour cometh, when ye shall neither in this mountain, nor yet at Jerusalem, worship the Father.**
>
> **John 4:21**

The key phrase in what Jesus told the woman at the well is **For the Father seeketh such to worship him** (John 4:23). He said "true worshippers" are those who worship in spirit and in truth, and those are the ones the Father seeks.

In checking the word *worship* in that verse, I found it to be a continuous action verb, which means that God is seeking one who worships Him continually. [Zodhiates, Spiros. *The Hebrew-Greek Key Study Bible, King James Version* (Grand Rapids: Baker Book House, 1984), pp. 1285, 1568.] God does not seek the saint who worships only on Sundays, in a certain place or at a certain time. He seeks those who worship in spirit and in truth continually.

If true worshippers are worshipping continually, then where does the New Testament place most of the emphasis? The New Testament emphasizes *praise* at a public gathering more than it does *worship*. However, if we are to be continually worshipping, this certainly would include Sundays or whatever days we gather together.

> **And it came to pass, while he blessed them, he was parted from them, and carried up into heaven.**
>
> **And they worshipped him and returned to Jerusalem with great joy:**
>
> **And were continually in the temple, praising and blessing God. Amen.**
>
> **Luke 24:51-53**

When the Pharisees asked Jesus to rebuke His followers for rejoicing and praising Him during His triumphal procession into Jerusalem a few days before the crucifixion, He answered that if He rebuked the people and they stopped, the stones would immediately cry out. The Phillips Translation says:

> **The stones in the road would cry out.**
>
> **Luke 19:40**

In Acts 16:15, an earthquake caused by God to free Paul and Silas from prison was in response to their praising.

First Peter 2:9 teaches that we are a royal priesthood to show forth the praises of Him who called us out of darkness into His marvellous light.

Perhaps Hebrews 13:15 NKJV puts the glorious cap on this emphasis on praise. We are to offer **the sacrifice of praise continually, which is the fruit of our lips giving thanks to His name.** [Literally, "making confession," marginal note.]

This verse teaches that there cannot be a true spirit of praise without a true spirit of thanksgiving, and this truth would certainly carry over into our times of worship. It stands to reason that there is no logic to praise and worship if we are not thankful to the One we praise and worship.

It is vital to teach our congregations all the Bible has to say about praise and worship and then practice what we learn in church services. But it is also vital that believers understand that if they do not worship God in everything they do, praising Him at all times, they could become highly religious but never develop a close relationship with Jesus nor a true awareness of the reality of the presence of God.

Worship from a heart of obedience does not build Christian character; however, Christians of true character will worship continually.

# 9

# Prosperity

Perhaps no subject surfaces more often in the Church nowadays than prosperity. Prosperity is a great Bible truth which seems to end in a ditch most of the time. On one extreme are those who are totally against prosperity being taught to any extent. On the other are those who teach and emphasize that every Christian ought to be prosperous to the extent of opulence.

Is it possible that much misunderstanding results from the misuse of terminology? The most appropriate word to describe one who is prosperous should be the word *blessed*. God said to Abraham:

> **That in blessing I will bless thee, and in multiplying I will multiply thy seed as the stars of the heaven, and as the sand which is upon the sea shore; and thy seed shall possess the gate of his enemies.**
> **Genesis 22:17**

One could be prosperous in material things, but that would not necessarily be the blessing of God or His prosperity. Deuteronomy 28:2 amplifies this word:

> **And all these blessings shall come on thee, and overtake thee, if thou shalt hearken unto the voice of the Lord thy God.**

*In the Bible, prosperity is described as being blessed in every aspect of life, not just material things.*

One could, by faith, confess prosperity for his household but be out of God's perfect will. Israel sought and got a king (Saul), but was out of God's perfect will. (See 1 Samuel 8.) Just because one owns a very expensive car and lives in a mansion does not always mean he is blessed of God or in His will.

A congregation, by its size and the generous giving of its members, could make a pastor very wealthy. This does not necessarily mean that God has blessed him or that he is in God's perfect will. Material wealth does not solely identify the blessing of God. Many leaders of cults have a very wealthy, affluent lifestyle.

Proverbs 10:22 AMP sheds a very interesting light on this subject.

> **The blessing of the Lord, it makes [truly] rich, and He adds no sorrow with it, neither does toiling increase it.**

One can, through his own efforts and strength, make himself rich in material wealth, yet not have God's blessing on him.

> **There is that maketh himself rich, yet hath nothing: there is that maketh himself poor, yet hath great riches.**
> **Proverbs 13:7**

The Hebrew word, *Shalom,* seems to express the meaning of prosperity as God views it. That word describes "happiness, peace, and health." One certainly cannot be happy and at peace if he cannot pay his bills and take adequate care of his family.

God blessed Israel as long as they obeyed Him and kept His commandments. Galatians 3:14 says:

> **That the blessing of Abraham might come on the Gentiles through Jesus Christ; that we might receive the promise of the Spirit through faith.**

The way Israel was blessed when they served God is comparable to the blessings that God desires for His people under the New Covenant.

# The Blessings of Abraham Are Ours

Those in the extreme ditch of poverty on one side and those in the extreme ditch of prosperity on the other, censuring each other, must come to a proper balance.

Our Lord Jesus repeatedly warned more people about loving the riches of earth than he did about them being in danger of going to hell. Yet the Word of God is very clear that, when a believer obeys the Word and lives a holy life, they can expect to be blessed in every way. We are in line for the same blessings as Abraham received if we live holy and tithe, as Abraham did.

The Bible does not teach, "Give, and it shall be taken away from you."

Third John 2 does not say, "Beloved, I wish above all things that you would be sick and poor."

Matthew 6:33 does not say, "Seek first the kingdom of God, and all these things shall be taken away from you."

However, the misuse and abuse of these scriptures has repelled many people and been a great detriment to the Church. Many preachers and evangelists have taken these same scriptures, along with others, and they have taught that all who tithe and give will be prospered as they themselves have been prospered. They leave a strong suggestion that if you fail to experience this same prosperity, you are lacking in faith and obedience.

One incident during our pastoral experience serves to illustrate this. We hosted an evangelist in our church, primarily because ours was the largest building available for his city-wide meeting. His method of taking an offering was, "If you do not have enough faith to empty your pocketbook or wallet in this offering, you may not have enough faith to be saved."

When my people (some of them old-age pensioners) asked me about this, I said, "Give what the Lord tells you to give without succumbing to pressure." Paul admonishes us in 2 Corinthians 9:7 to give as our heart leads us, not out of pressure from men, but out of love for and obedience to God, who loves a cheerful giver.

The admonition by the Apostle Paul in 1 Timothy 6:12 is to be fighting continually the good fight of faith. He followed that with a warning to those who always are striving to be richer:

**For the love of money is the root of all evil.**

This is a strong warning against coveting the things of this world: whether it is confessing for a wealthy, affluent lifestyle enjoyed by the "jet set" or mansions, expensive automobiles, dinners in the best restaurants, and so forth.

In his second letter to Timothy, the Apostle Paul related how his life was ending successfully, because he had "fought the good fight of faith." Paul had experienced all of the pitfalls of a successful ministry.

The pitfall he wanted most to overcome was coveting the things of this world. Because of his background, Paul was entitled to a high position in life and probably could have had anything he wanted materially.

All this is brought out in Romans 7:7,8, where Paul confessed he had once been guilty of covetousness. The commandment, **Thou shalt not covet** (Exodus 20:17), defeated him, and he determined that he would never again allow covetousness to overpower him.

Many great, successful pastors and ministers have failed to fight the good fight of faith. To be blessed of God and have all of our needs supplied as the Bible promises brings great joy, but with it comes an awesome responsibility to stay out of the ditches that lay just outside of the boundaries of sound doctrine.

Those ministers and pastors who seldom mention the return of Jesus Christ (the Rapture) must be careful that they are not enjoying the prosperity with which God has blessed them so much that they no longer get excited about Jesus' returning. The last church in the third chapter of Revelation is referred to as a very prosperous people who became so caught up in things that they missed His coming.

God's blessings bring continual peace and health even as Abraham experienced. He was obedient, gave generously, and was not covetous like his nephew, Lot, who *was* covetous and chose the affluent lifestyle of Sodom.

## Keeping Priorities Straight

Where is the balance to be found? Certainly not in the left ditch of poverty and need. On the other hand, most assuredly balance is not to be found in the right ditch of coveting excessive affluence and opulent lifestyles.

The middle of the Gospel road is to make it our first priority to seek such a relationship with the Lord that there will be no thought of covetousness, about which God said, **Thou shalt not.** Our purpose must be to fight continually the good fight of faith so that we never become a victim of insatiable greed.

Paul, in 1 Timothy 6:5, warned his young friend:

> **Perverse disputings of men of corrupt minds, and destitute of the truth, supposing that gain is godliness: from such withdraw thyself.**

He was warning Timothy not to allow appearances to deceive him into believing that riches always represent the blessing of God.

The late Smith Wigglesworth, that great apostle of faith, never confessed for riches. He believed that God would supply his need, but he never coveted an affluent lifestyle. He was convinced that to covet to be rich would only open the door for Satan to enter.

He said once, "There is one thing I am very grateful to the Lord for, and that is that He has given me grace not to have a desire for money."

It is so regrettable that many great men of God, who once had a supernatural ministry, now have fallen (and many more are in danger of falling) into the ditch to which the coveting of an opulent lifestyle has brought them. Worse still are those who truly believe that material wealth and possessions is a standard for spirituality, **that gain is godliness.**

It is my hope that this admonition of the Apostle Paul to "fight the good fight of faith" will take on a new meaning to us all, and that we will, more than ever before, recognize the "wiles of the devil" that seek to minimize and destroy valid ministries through a love of money.

Yes, God wants us to prosper and be in health, but only as our soul prospers. (3 John 2.) Our soul prospers when we keep our eyes on Him, covet an intimate relationship with Him more than anything else, obey Him in thought, word, and deed, and thus keep the faith.

# 10

# Eschatology

In terms of diversity and extremes of opinions, there is no other subject in Christendom that rivals the subject of eschatology (the doctrine of end times). The ditches of faulty doctrine about this subject are so deep, it seems almost futile to try to rescue those who are entrenched in them.

The controversy has always centered on two issues: the rapture or catching away of the Church to Heaven and the return of the Lord Jesus Christ to earth to rule and reign. Even when the Church was in its infancy the subject was discussed passionately. Second Peter 3:3,4 NKJV is Peter's warning about end times. He prophesied that there would be those in the last days who would deny and laugh at the idea that Jesus would return, treating this doctrine of the faith as a myth.

> scoffers will come in the last days, walking according to their own lusts,
>
> and saying, "Where is the promise of His coming? For since the fathers fell asleep, all things continue as they were from the beginning of creation."

Scripture attests to the fact that Jesus will return for His saints in the rapture, or catching away (1 Thessalonians 4:13-18), and that He will later come back with His saints (Revelation 19:11-16). The only fact that has been unknown to the Church are the exact dates. Jesus said, **Watch therefore, for ye know neither the day nor the hour wherein the Son of man cometh** (Matthew 25:13).

The scoffers Peter mentioned are still present today. This group mocks the mention of the subject of the Lord's return. These believers spiritualize every prophecy, making time a continuum without ages or seasons.

On the other extreme, we have the group who so zealously proclaim the coming of the Lord that they are continually setting dates for His arrival. These are the extreme dispensationalists, who have every epoch of time figured out nearly to the minute.

Although Jesus did teach about His return and that this event would be seen by all on earth (Matthew 24:30), one thing must be understood. He could teach very little to the Jews about the day of grace for the Gentiles or anything to do with the Church. If He had taught publicly about the coming Church, when Gentiles would receive salvation without the law and without circumcision, such teaching would have been immediately and violently rejected by all, including the twelve disciples.

To have taught further on the subject of grace, the rapture, and the resurrection of dead saints with the living (1 Corinthians 15:51-54) would have been far beyond the Jews' ability to understand and accept. Later on, after the cross, resurrection, ascension, birth of the Church at Pentecost, and the addition of Gentiles to the Church, the Apostle Paul could teach them more fully concerning these truths.

## The Rapture of the Church

One of the clearest Scripture passages which describes the departure of the Church to Heaven is found in 1 Corinthians 15:52-55,58:

> Behold, I shew you a mystery; We shall not all sleep, but we shall all be changed,
>
> In a moment, in the twinkling of an eye, at the last trump: for the trumpet shall sound, and the dead shall be raised incorruptible, and we shall be changed.

> For this corruptible must put on incorruption, and this mortal must put on immortality.
>
> So when this corruptible shall have put on incorruption, and this mortal shall have put on immortality, then shall be brought to pass the saying that is written, Death is swallowed up in victory.
>
> Therefore, my beloved brethren, be ye stedfast, unmoveable, always abounding in the work of the Lord, forasmuch as ye know that your labour is not in vain in the Lord.

I added verse 58 to make the point that Paul admonishes the Corinthians that because they know they will one day depart this earth, they should be motivated to be stable, productive Christians. The Apostle John reiterates this in 1 John 3:2,3:

> Beloved, now are we the sons of God, and it doth not yet appear what we shall be: but we know that, when he shall appear, we shall be like him; for we shall see him as he is.
>
> And every man that hath this hope in him purifieth himself, even as he is pure.

John is describing the rapture of the Church—when Jesus shall appear, bring us to His side, and we shall "be like Him." He goes on to say that all believers who have the hope of the rapture will continually be mindful of how they live their lives, purifying themselves.

*The rapture is not an excuse to live any way we feel, but the inspiration to live in total surrender to Jesus Christ and to accomplish His will while we are here on earth.*

The problem which arises on the subject of the rapture comes with a mistranslation of the Greek word *apostasia* in 2 Thessalonians. Let's look at this passage in the *King James Version:*

> Now we beseech you, brethren, by the coming of our Lord Jesus Christ, and by our gathering together unto him,

> That ye be not soon shaken in mind, or be troubled, neither by spirit, nor by word, nor by letter as from us, as that the day of Christ is at hand.
>
> Let no man deceive you by any means: for that day shall not come, except there come a falling away *(apostasia)* first, and that man of sin be revealed, the son of perdition.
>
> **2 Thessalonians 2:1-3**

The word *apostasia* literally means to leave or depart. Here is how Kenneth Wuest translates verse 3:

> Do not begin to allow anyone to lead you astray in any way, because that day shall not come except the aforementioned departure [of the Church to heaven] comes first and the man of the lawlessness is disclosed [in his true identity], the son of perdition.

Some theologians say that just prior to the Lord's return there will be a great falling away *from the faith,* what they term the great apostasy. This gives them the excuse to reject the tremendous movements within and growth of the Church among those who do not believe the way they do.

For example, some evangelicals label the Charismatics as apostates because they speak in tongues and practice the gifts of the Spirit in their services. To the evangelical world, then, this outpouring of God's Spirit and great harvest of souls into the kingdom of God becomes no more than a sign that Jesus is coming back soon, because the Charismatic Movement is apostasy, false and of the devil. The same thing was said of Pentecostals in the early days of this century.

Those who ascribe to the view that there will be a mass exodus of believers from the faith just before Jesus returns are looking for apostasy, not renewal and a tremendous harvest. Furthermore, if the Lord Jesus is going to come back for a backslidden, apostate Church, He already has missed greater opportunities! Many times in history the Church has waxed and waned, becoming almost extinct at times. One such period was the thousand years from 500 to 1500 A.D., called "the Dark Ages."

It is also very clear that "falling away" does not teach a spiritual decline but a departure because of the verses following verse 3, which speak of the revealing of the antichrist. Again, let's take a look at the Wuest translation of 2 Thessalonians 2:5-7:

> Do you not remember that while I was still with you I kept on telling you these things? And now you know with a positive assurance that which [namely, the departure of the Church, the saints being assembled together to the Lord] is preventing his being disclosed [as to his true identity].

Paul is telling us that until the Church is taken out of the earth, the antichrist cannot be revealed. This makes perfect sense, because an apostate Church would never hinder the antichrist. Only a strong, vibrant Church would hold him back.

## The Second Coming

The second *coming* of Jesus Christ to earth is often confused with His *appearing* at the rapture. At the rapture of the Church, we have seen from Scripture that believers will rise to meet Him *in the air.* He will appear only to His own. All the world will see is that multitudes who have professed Jesus Christ as their Lord and Savior have suddenly disappeared off the face of the earth! Later, Jesus will return to rule and reign on earth.

The controversy regarding the second coming is mostly related to when He is coming back. Most Christians believe He is coming back, but the conflict is over when: before, during, or after the tribulation. And there are those who do not believe in a literal seven-year tribulation period or a literal thousand-year (millenial) reign.

Some teach that the Church will go through the seven-year period prior to Christ's return called "the Great Tribulation," or "the time of Jacob's trouble." After our study in 2 Thessalonians, chapter 2, we can see how this is false. But if it is taught that we must go through this, it would certainly influence believers to be looking for the appearance of the antichrist more than Christ. Furthermore, if the Church were to have to go through the tribulation, then there is certainly no need right now to get excited about Jesus' coming!

For a wonderful explanation of the various viewpoints concerning the second coming, I recommend that you read the section of the *Spirit-Filled Life Study Bible* (Nashville: Thomas Nelson Inc.) that precedes the book of Revelation. These "different positions" include:

- The premillenial pretribulation view

- The premillenial posttribulation view

- The premillenial midtribulation view

- The premillenial pretribulation partial-rapture view

- The premillenial prewrath of God rapture view

- The evangelical postmillenial view

- The amillennial view (dating from Augustine, about 500 A.D.)

- Another amillennial view

Just reading the list of all the different views may be discouraging! However, always keep in mind that these various viewpoints concerning when Jesus will return are not "heaven or hell" issues. The danger of falling into a ditch here would be to take one of these viewpoints so seriously as to become a spiritual bigot toward others who believe differently, thus causing strife and division among the brethren.

The important point to remember is that Jesus is coming back and He told us to be ready!

# The Danger of Spiritualizing

If one was to endeavor to give a simple explanation of how confusion entered into the teaching of end times, it would have to be laid at the door of "spiritualizing."

*To spiritualize means to take a literal Bible truth and give it a spiritual meaning only.*

My favorite quote on this subject is: "Take a great truth and give it a meaning God didn't know about." A good example of this kind of spiritualizing is found in some interpretations of Revelation 20:1-3 NKJV:

> **Then I saw an angel coming down from heaven, having the key of the bottomless pit and a great chain in his hand.**
>
> **And he laid hold of the dragon, that serpent of old, who is the Devil and Satan, and bound him for a thousand years;**
>
> **and He cast him into the bottomless pit, and shut him up, and set a seal upon him, so that he should deceive the nations no more till the thousand years were finished. But after these things he must be released for a little while.**

Those who believe the above verses are not describing a literal event to happen in the future have built a doctrine around it called *amillennialism,* which means there is no thousand-year period of Christ's reign on earth, but that the term "a thousand years" simply means a long period of indefinite time.

It is true that there are many places in the Bible where the writers used figures of speech that were not meant to be taken literally but were used to illustrate truth. A good example of this is found in Matthew 5:29,30 NKJV:

"If your right eye causes you to sin, pluck it out and cast it from you; for it is more profitable for you that one of your members perish, than for your whole body to be cast into hell.

"And if your right hand causes you to sin, cut it off and cast it from you; for it is more profitable for you that one of your members perish, than for your whole body to be cast into hell.

Literally "plucking out your eye" or "cutting off your hand" is not what Jesus meant. He was using a figure of speech familiar to the Jews, illustrating the importance of getting rid of any areas in your life that offend God.

This is not really a difficult passage of Scripture, and I have never known anyone who misinterpreted it. The disciples certainly understood the meaning behind this phrase, because when Simon Peter cursed Jesus and denied that he even knew him during the hours before the crucifixion, he did not go out and cut out his tongue!

It is quite another matter to spiritualize away a thousand years! In the book of Revelation a thousand-year period is mentioned six times, and we can tell from the context that it is not a figure of speech, a fabrication, or a fiction.

The doctrine of amillennialism comes from a very illogical interpretation of Scripture. If one could say there will not be a literal thousand-year period when Satan is bound, just as those verses say, then it would be equally possible to say that "Satan" is a figure of speech and does not exist, or that there is no such place as a "bottomless pit."

# Spiritualizing Leads
# to Incorrect Theology

If one subscribes to a spiritualized interpretation of end-time prophecies in the Bible, then rest assured it will affect interpretations of other areas of Bible doctrine. For example, those who have rejected the simple teaching of the Apostle Paul concerning the rapture will often be found lacking in understanding of other great literal Bible truths, such as continuing to purify their lives and winning the lost.

Much post-millennial teaching usually is associated with what is known as "Kingdom Now" theology, which teaches that Jesus is waiting for His Body to get the world saved and for the Church to become perfected, *then* He will set up His eternal kingdom on this earth. This view leaves little room for the rapture and is very legalistic in nature. One must quickly reject this approach as being unscriptural.

First, the Bible does not teach that we will win the entire world or completely occupy it. It teaches that the world will wax worse and worse.

> **This know also, that in the last days perilous times shall come.**
>
> **For men shall be lovers of their own selves, covetous, boasters, proud, blasphemers, disobedient to parents, unthankful, unholy,**
>
> **Without natural affection, truce breakers, false accusers, incontinent** (without restraint) **fierce, despisers of those that are good,**
>
> **Traitors, heady, highminded, lovers of pleasures more than lovers of God;**
>
> **Having a form of godliness, but denying the power thereof: from such turn away.**
>
> **2 Timothy 3:1-5**

Can anyone deny this aptly describes the time in which we are living? Jesus described the society of the days just before His return as comparable to those of the decadent days of Lot and the days of Noah. (Matthew 24:37,38.)

Another verse that has been used to teach that the Lord Jesus is waiting for the Church to bring in the harvest before He returns is James 5:7 AMP. [Also, see Wycliffe's Translation, p. 1438.]

> **So be patient, brethren, [as you wait] till the coming of the Lord. See how the *farmer* waits expectantly for the precious harvest from the land. [See how] he keeps up his patient [vigil] over it until it receives the early and late rains.**

In checking all of the available commentaries at my disposal, I found they all agree that the"farmer," symbolizes the saints waiting for the judgment of God on the enemies of righteousness.

If you read the first seven verses of James 5 for the context, James is acknowledging how the evil enemies of God have seemed to prosper over believers. Then he cites the case of the farmer who waits for the precious fruit of the earth. This teaches that, with patience, we wait for Jesus' return, when He will not only take us home but will also avenge His persecuted saints.

Second, if the Church must be perfected on this earth before Christ can return, then what did the dead saints do to be ready? They are going to rise *first* when the trumpet sounds! Here is what they did to be ready: *They died in Christ!* The phrase "in Christ" is all the perfecting one is going to need. (1 Thessalonians 4:16,17.)

Ephesians 5:27, which describes the Church as without "spot or wrinkle," tells how we appear *in His sight,* not how we appear *to each other.* Jesus is not waiting for us to become perfected human beings on this earth before He returns. A resounding no! *We are waiting for Him.* The time set for His coming is His business, not ours. (Romans 8:23; 1 Corinthians 1:7; and 2 Thessalonians 3:5.)

To say Christ cannot return because 1) the world must first be won to Christ, and 2) the Church is not yet perfected, is to lead saints to become so involved in "winning" and "perfecting" that they neglect the one thing Jesus emphasized again and again, which was to "be ready."

With this view of end times, the focus of the Christian life is transferred from God's grace to our works, taking our eyes off Jesus and looking to ourselves. We have taken the burden of history from the sovereign hand of God and put it in the Church's hands. Let us not forget that even Noah, after building the ark which would save him from the flood, stood in helpless wonder when he realized only God could shut the door to keep the water out! (See Genesis 7:16.)

A well-known pastor said on television recently, "I do not believe Christ will come in my lifetime because the Church is not ready." First of all, who can judge if and when the Church is ready?

Yes, we are admonished by the New Testament writers to be ready, but our being ready or not has nothing to do with when Jesus will return. If we believe our being ready is the determining factor of Jesus' return, we are taking on a responsibility that can only be God's.

Repeating statements like this also causes Christians to think that Jesus might not return for years; therefore, it makes no difference how they live. They become lax in their commitment to Christ. We have already seen clearly that the passages of Scripture on the rapture include that this is our inspiration to live godly lives.

In 1 John 3:2,3, the Apostle John says that all believers who have the hope of the rapture will continually be mindful of how they live their lives, purifying themselves. Therefore, it stands to reason that those who do not believe in the rapture and do not have this hope may not care how they live their lives or whether or not they are purifying themselves, because they have no anticipation of Jesus' appearing.

# The Key Is To Be Ready

This "waiting for our Lord's return" is not to be used to wait around and do nothing. We, as saints, are "to occupy" (work). We are to be active in spreading the Gospel around the world. In my fifty years of ministry, I have never met a group of saints who believed in the soon coming of Jesus who sat around doing nothing! A strong expectancy dictates strong effort!

Jesus said in Matthew 24:36 that no one knows the day and hour of His return except the Father. Not even the angels know! This confirms that *the hour has already been set,* and we are to be ready.

We can read the prophecies and see the signs of the times, but in no way do we have license to set a date for His coming. I have tried to warn of taking extreme positions. *Extreme* means "the utmost removal from that which is reasonable and sane."

*No one* can prove a position on this subject that would be beyond question. The best thing we can do as Christians is to refuse to allow these positions to influence us to ignore the strong warnings of the Lord Jesus to *be ready*.

Do not allow the confusion about this subject to lead you into a ditch. Refuse to let the many opinions, books, and articles that have been written bewilder you. Rise up and say, "The one thing I do know for certain is that Jesus *is* coming back, and I am going to be ready!"

In more than three hundred places in the scriptures, it is made very clear that Jesus Christ, our Lord, will return to earth. Any teaching or position on this important and exciting subject that confuses saints must be considered as being unbalanced — especially if that position weakens the truth that all saints should be ready for Christ's return.

The teaching that Jesus cannot return "until" something happens overlooks the admonition of the

Apostle Paul in 1 Corinthians 15:52 that we shall be caught up in the air and changed in a split second of time. Flesh will be changed to spirit so fast, there will be no time to pray, repent, or get ready.

Reader, be ready! Here are three guidelines that may help you to remember this:

1. Go to bed ready.

2. Arise to meet each new day ready.

3. Be looking for His coming throughout each day.

[For further reading and study, I would recommend the two books which I have written on this subject (also published by Harrison House): *Another Look at the Rapture* and *Final Days and Counting*. The latter book also contains some instructions for those who miss the rapture.]

# 11

# Prophets

While there are many ditches to avoid, none is more misleading and crippling to the young believer than the lack of understanding concerning the ministry or function of prophets. The Bible gives many warnings to believers about false prophets, and for good reason. We have seen quite a few of them bring death and destruction in the last few decades.

For example, not too long ago, the news media was broadcasting the story of a group of Christians barricaded in a commune in Waco, Texas. Most of these misguided souls senselessly gave their lives for a self-styled prophet.

Just a few years before this, another group of Christians followed their leader to a foreign country and ultimately to their deaths, believing that he spoke for God as a prophet.

In the 1940s, there was a group who were followers of such a prophet until his premature death. Even today there are people who believe he will be brought back to be greatly used of God. They gather in groups and listen to messages he preached while he was alive.

Some false prophets are famous or have a large following, but many others don't necessarily have a following but make it their business to be telling everyone what they should be doing or what is going on in their lives. They call themselves prophets, but they are false. They are either ignorant to what a true prophet is, or they are operating by demonic power instead of the Holy Spirit.

# Who Are You Listening To?

In the Old Testament, believers were not born again. They did not have the Holy Spirit residing inside them, nor did they have the Word of God in many cases. Thus they relied a great deal on the prophets to hear from God.

But today, through Jesus Christ, we have the Comforter and Teacher living in our hearts and the Bible to turn to for the knowledge of God's will.

> **For as many as are led by the spirit of God, they are the sons of God.**
>
> **Romans 8:14**

> **But be ye doers of the word, and not hearers only, deceiving your own selves.**
>
> **James 1:22**

In Acts 13:1-3, it is stated that Paul and Barnabas were sent forth into missionary work by the Holy Spirit. No prophet's name is mentioned as being personally responsible for their commissioning, nor could any other person be credited for this direction. The Holy Spirit is acknowledged as being responsible.

When we have a decision to make, if it is general, we can find principles in Scripture which will determine God's will in a situation. On the other hand, if it is something specific, we can ask the Holy Spirit.

For example, you do not have to ask the Holy Spirit if you should work. The Bible says in 2 Thessalonians 3:10 that if you don't work you don't eat, and in 1 Timothy 5:8 that if you do not provide for your family you are worse than an infidel.

On the other hand, if you have two job offers and you are confused about which one is God's will, there is no Scripture reference which says, "Jim should go to work for the company that has offered him a company car." Only the Holy Spirit can direct you in this situation.

In the midst of a trying situation or crisis, God may lead you to seek the counsel of another believer or a minister, and that believer or minister may give you a word of wisdom, word of knowledge, or prophecy. Or, God may lead another believer or minister to you to deliver His Word or a specific word to you from Him.

In either case, where many believers make a mistake is assuming everything the "prophet" has said will come true exactly as they said it and that it is scriptural. Instead of listening to the Holy Spirit on the inside of them for confirmation and studying the issue out in the Word of God to make sure it is sound doctrinally, they blindly begin to live their life according to it.

Another place where believers go astray is by *seeking* a word of prophecy for everything they must decide instead of listening to the Holy Spirit and studying God's Word. The danger in living the Christian life this way is that we can open ourselves up to the deception of the enemy, as Paul and James say in the verses we just quoted. If we do not live by God's Word and His Spirit, we deceive ourselves and are not living as sons of God.

Does the New Testament proclaim the necessity of a prophetic ministry to give Christians personal direction? Yes — if it confirms something already given them in their spirits by the Holy Spirit and the Word of God.

It is my sincere desire that weak or newborn Christians will give time to the study of God's Word in order to build up their inner man to the point that they can rely upon the Holy Spirit for direction. Until they reach that level of maturity, however, they need all the help they can get from mature Christians.

The reason it is so important for new believers to be taught how to know the will and direction of God for their lives is obvious. Just look around you and see the cases of sincere, Bible-believing saints who have made incredible leaps of faith into failure on what they thought was God's word, but was really man's vain imaginings.

One family sells all their earthly possessions and moves to a mission field on the other side of the world based upon the word of a so-called prophet, then loses everything because they were out of God's will.

People have gotten married on a supposed "word from God" given to them by some well-meaning brother or sister, only to discover later and after much pain and anguish that they were out of the will of God.

Some believers have been prophesied over in public that they were committing adultery, and the "words" were simply false accusations.

Saints, by personal prophecy, have been challenged to give large amounts to ministries or even certain individuals. Some have dipped into their savings, and many have lost what they had.

As in every decision we make, we are to give in obedience to the Word and the Holy Spirit's leading, not from the pressure of men. We listen respectfully and politely to those who have a word for us, but our ultimate source of guidance is the Word and the Spirit, which are always in agreement. (1 John 5:8.)

## How To Spot a False Prophet

What marked a false prophet in the Old Testament was inaccuracy and leading the people away from God. The prophet had to be one hundred percent correct on every prophecy he gave and lead the people to God, or else they were killed.

**"But that prophet or that dreamer of dreams shall be put to death, because he has spoken in order to turn you away from the Lord your God, who brought you**

out of the land of Egypt and redeemed you from the house of bondage, to entice you from the way in which the Lord your God commanded you to walk. So you shall put (exterminate) away the evil from your midst.

**Deuteronomy 13:5 NKJV**

And if thou say in thine heart, How shall we know the word which the Lord hath not spoken?

When a prophet speaketh in the name of the Lord, if the thing follow not, nor come to pass, that is the thing which the Lord hath not spoken, but the prophet hath spoken it presumptuously: thou shalt not be afraid of him.

**Deuteronomy 18:21-22**

The New Testament does not command false prophets to be killed, but it has a lot to say about them and repeatedly warns us of them. Jesus told us that we would not know them by how they looked, that the wolves would come in sheeps' clothing, but that we could spot them by how they lived their lives.

Beware of false prophets, which come to you in sheep's clothing, but inwardly they are ravening wolves.

Ye shall know them by their fruits. Do men gather grapes of thorns, or figs of thistles?

Even so every good tree bringeth forth good fruit; but a corrupt tree bringeth forth evil fruit.

A good tree cannot bring forth evil fruit, neither can a corrupt tree bring forth good fruit.

Every tree that bringeth not forth good fruit is hewn down, and cast into the fire.

Wherefore by their fruits ye shall know them.

**Matthew 7:15-20**

Does the man or woman who claims to be a prophet walk in the integrity of the Word of God? Do you see the fruit of the Spirit working in their life? Are they consistently correct in their prophecies, and do those prophecies bring forth the fruit of righteousness in those to whom they minister? Do they point you to God and not to themselves?

In Ephesians 4:11,12 we have the key scripture reference for this subject.

> **And he gave some, apostles; and some, prophets; and some, evangelists; and some, pastors and teachers;**
>
> **For the perfecting of the saints, for the work of the ministry, for the edifying of the body of Christ.**

God has set some prophets in the Body of Christ to help us mature in Christ and do the work of the ministry He has called us to do. Furthermore, there are many believers who move in the word of wisdom, word of knowledge, and prophecy — all three being gifts of the Holy Spirit to the Church to accomplish the same end. (1 Corinthians 12:7-11.)

We find several examples of prophets and prophetic ministry in the New Testament. In Acts 21:8-12, disciples prophesied to Paul through the Holy Spirit the trials and tribulation he would encounter if he went to Jerusalem. Because of the prophecy, they begged him not to go. This is a good example of saints using prophecy to attempt to give personal direction.

In the end, whether it was right or wrong, Paul felt compelled to continue on to Jerusalem. He suffered just as it had been prophesied he would. One of those who warned him was a believer named Agabus, whom the Scripture labels a prophet.

> **And as we tarried there many days, there came down from Judaea a certain prophet, named Agabus.**
>
> **Acts 21:10**
>
> **And there stood up one of them named Agabus, and signified by the Spirit that there should be great dearth throughout all the world: which came to pass in the days of Claudius Caesar.**
>
> **Acts 11:28**

Prophets and prophecy function only to serve God's purpose, which is to help believers do His will in the earth. They are never to aggrandize any person — which brings us to another way you can spot a false prophet.

Many false prophets work through demons or familiar spirits, which will always ultimately glorify man and not God. A *familiar* spirit is just what its name implies: it knows all about and is familiar with the person who is receiving the prophecy.

This demon will know personal, private things, such as the kind of house in which you live, what kind of pets you have, intimate details about your family, your doctor's name, and so forth, and can describe in detail many confidential conversations you have had. The false prophet merely passes this information on to the believer.

One well-known prophet told a lady that she had a letter in her purse from her son in the Navy, and he proceeded to tell her word for word what was in the letter. Such minute details should cause one to be alert! Jesus Himself did not give great detail when guiding and directing the disciples prophetically.

Jesus instructed the disciples about a man they were to follow in order to have a room in which to celebrate the Passover the night before He was crucified, but He only gave enough information to get the job done. (Luke 22:10.)

He called Nathaniel "a man without guile," and Nathaniel wanted to know how Jesus knew him, because they had just met for the first time. Jesus said:

> . . . **Before that Philip called thee, when thou wast under the fig tree, I saw thee.**
>
> **John 1:48**

Jesus did not describe how Nathaniel was dressed or any other intimate details about His past life. He only gave enough information to get the point across. The bare essentials said enough to verify He was a prophet.

Jesus told Peter He would deny Him three times before the "cock" crew the next morning, but He did not give Peter any more details.

When Jesus told the disciples at the Passover meal that one of them would betray Him, and they asked which one, He simply said, "The one to whom I give the 'sop.'"

When modern prophets go beyond essential information and attempt to give many *nonessential* details, they open themselves up to a different spirit. In disclosing specific, unnecessary details, they are merely enhancing their own image before a congregation. This is leading the people away from God to themselves.

One pastor I know described an incident where a "prophetess" was accurately calling people out of the congregation by name. Some men in the church began to notice that she came early to the services and moved among the people in the sanctuary, paying close attention to Bibles (with the owners' names on them) left to save seats for the next service.

She was memorizing the names of these people and would later call them to come forward for ministry. These men were indignant that this error was being manifested in their midst. So they brought Bibles with names of people who no longer attended there and placed them on seats! Thus, the "prophetess" was exposed as false.

In Acts 13:6, a false prophet is identified as operating through sorcery, or the power of familiar spirits. Moses wrote in Leviticus 20:27 to put to death a man or woman who was a "medium," or someone who operated by familiar spirits. It was said of King Saul (the first king of Israel) that he had put away out of the land of Israel all such who had a familiar spirit. (1 Samuel 18; also, 2 Kings 23:24 and 1 Chronicles 10:13.)

*Strong's Concordance* has this definition of the Hebrew word translated in English as *a familiar spirit*: "a mumble, i.e., a water skin (from its hollow sound); hence a necromancer (ventriloquist, as from a jar): — bottle." ["Hebrew and Chaldee Dictionary," #178, p. 9. Also see the *Jamieson, Fausset, and Brown Commentary*, Vol. 1, p. 205, which shows the term as related to "ventriloquist."]

Our understanding of the word *ventriloquist* is "one who speaks for another person." The one spoken through, as a puppet, gives out words that have been put in its mouth by the one operating it. The same familiar spirits who caused some Old Testament prophets to go astray are the same who speak through false prophets, mediums, and "channelers" today.

Can Christians be deceived and allow demons to operate through them prophetically? Absolutely! Christians have a will and can choose whether God or the devil will rule their hearts and minds. God has grace for those who are truly deceived and ignorant, and He will move Heaven and earth to set them free, but great destruction will come to those who willfully grieve the Holy Spirit in this way.

It is very evident that the New Testament has explicit warnings about false prophets, and they are just as stern and as strong as those in the Old Testament. In over fifteen biblical references, we are warned about them.

Obviously, if it was impossible for a Christian to be deceived by a false prophet, then the Bible misled us by warning us to "beware" of them!

A false prophet may not be easily discerned. However, they can be quickly identified and exposed if we are walking according to God's Word and His Spirit.

# Not All Signs and Wonders Are From God

All of us have been made aware, along with the general public, of national ministries that have been exposed as false during the past few years. In one instance, a minister had a tiny receiver in his ear through which he was receiving information from his wife about various individuals. The wife was reading cards which these people had previously filled out. People were being deceived into believing this was prophetic knowledge from God.

We are talking here about practices that are not orthodox, so we ask ourselves, "Does the New Testament record any unorthodox practices?"

Yes, it does. For example, in Acts 5:15, we are told that Peter's shadow healed people, and the healing was not through the efforts of Peter. However, there is not another mention of anyone being healed in this manner. Apparently, it was a one-time occurence. *You cannot make doctrines or practices based on one-time occurences.*

We all want the power of God to be manifested to set captives free, but we want this to happen in such a biblical way that God receives all of the glory and people follow Jesus. The ditch we fall into by getting our eyes on people and ministries could become a ditch of death.

The men and women doing these things may no doubt be sincere and doing what they feel God has led them to do. But sincerity will not protect anyone from error. Only knowledge of the Word of God and discernment from the Holy Spirit will enable you to "test" the spirits and know the true from the counterfeit.

We are to look to Jesus, not to His ministers and handmaidens. God cannot and will not share His glory with a human being. We have one hero, the Lord Jesus

Christ. We are well-taught in the Word of God to lift Jesus up and exalt His name above every name.

Never in the history of the Church has there been such an abundance of self-styled prophets. Reader, stay away from that dangerous ditch and caution other believers of the peril.

Remember: If a false prophet ministering in the power of a familiar spirit was obvious, Jesus would not have warned us to look out for them. He also said that false prophets, false teachers, and even false "Christs" will abound in these last days. Watch and pray that you enter not into this kind of deception!

Keep your eyes on and follow Jesus, the author and finisher of your faith (Hebrews 12:2), attend and become involved in a sound Bible-teaching church, listen to the voice of the Holy Spirit, and you will avoid falling into a ditch of false prophecy.

# 12

# Petitioning

When the spiritual renewal of the 1970s touched the youth of America, it was referred to as "the Jesus Movement." Newsweek and Time magazines get the credit for the phrasing that has become the de facto terminology in discussing this wonderful decade-long spiritual movement. The influence of this movement can still be felt through the thousands of young men and women who came to the Lord during that time and are now in positions of church leadership today.

Secular magazines could not help but refer to what was happening as a "Jesus Movement." Jesus appeared in every aspect of it — the art work, the songs, the teaching and preaching, and perhaps most importantly, the praying.

It surprises many to discover that this "Jesus emphasis" of the '70s also appears in every major revival involving the outpouring of the Holy Spirit. The genesis of the Pentecostal movement in America, for example, which quietly began in the late 1800s and exploded on the American scene in 1906 through the Azusa Street revival of Los Angeles, California, was entirely focused on Jesus. In reading the writings of that period, it is striking to notice the similarities with the emphasis of the '70s.

Why are these similarities important to notice? It is because both movements involve the ministry of the Holy Spirit breaking into the existent church structures and into the current secular cultures. Wherever the Holy Spirit ministers, the emphasis is always Jesus Christ.

In the early days of Pentecost, evangelists, pastors, and teachers, newly filled with the Holy Spirit, taught about Jesus, preached the gospel of Jesus, sang about Jesus, and prayed in Jesus' name. They did this almost exclusively. So much was their adoration for the Son, and the Father rarely was mentioned. It was not their intention to dishonor the Father. They simply were preoccupied with the revelation of the Son that filled their lives through the Holy Spirit.

This same phenomenon occurred in the "Jesus movement" of the '70s. Was there imbalance? Yes. In seasons of reformation, in times of renewal, there always have been counterbalance presentations which, when heard out of context, are extreme. Staying out of the ditch is nearly impossible — especially in the heat of revival! But continuing to live in ditches is not profitable and certainly not comfortable.

Some teaching that attempted to bring balance to the "Jesus emphasis" inadvertently created some very uncomfortable ditches. These ditches centered on prayer.

In the maturing years following the Pentecostal outpouring at the beginning of the century and in the years following the "Jesus movement," there were several attempts to bring balance to what was perceived as excess. In rare instances, some groups within the renewal movements became polarized, either teaching that one should never pray to Jesus or that one should only pray to Jesus — or only in Jesus' name.

One of the unfortunate teachings that encouraged people not to pray to Jesus also is quite innocent. The basis of the teaching is found in the midnight conversation Jesus had with His disciples on the eve of His crucifixion. Only John records this dialogue, which begins in chapter 13 and concludes with the intercession of chapter 17 and the betrayal in chapter 18.

Most of the dialogue centers around questions the disciples are asking. Their questions make for a study in themselves!

Thomas: "Would you show us the way?"

Philip: "Would you show us the Father?"

Judas: "How can we see you if no one else can?"

John's report of this midnight dialogue consists of the answers that Jesus gave to the troubled disciples. Not one of them understood what was really happening. Questions! They were full of questions. Then Peter made a declaration, full of honest intent, but lacking power.

"I will not fail You," he said.

In His answer, Jesus foretells Peter's failure and continues with a word of encouragement to all believers who find themselves with honest intent — yet powerless.

> **Let not your hearts be troubled: ye believe in God, believe also in me.**
>
> **In My Father's house are many mansions; if it were not so, I would have told you. I go to prepare a place for you.**
>
> **. . . That where I am, there ye may be also.**
>
> **John 14:1-3**

Thomas interrupts with his question, "We have no idea what this is all about — where you are going. How could we know the way?"

Remember? Jesus has just said, "That where I am, there you may be."

Thomas replies, "We need a map. We would love to be with you. But if we don't know where you are, how could we find you?"

In our language, Jesus' reply is, "You don't need a map. You need Me! I am the map. I am the way to the Father!"

Now comes Philip: "Show us the Father. That would satisfy our questions."

This brings a reproof from Jesus: "Have I been with you for so long, and you don't understand that when you hear Me, you are hearing the Father? When you see Me, you are seeing the Father. That is what My ministry is all about."

Questions. They are full of questions. And, when you finally arrive at John 16:23, they have just finished questioning yet again among themselves. "We can't figure out what He means . . . ."

To this, Jesus replies, "*When you finally see Me again*, you will ask no more questions."

This is the statement that is translated in the *King James Version* as **In that day ye will ask me nothing."** Unfortunately, it has been misconstrued to be associated with the statement immediately following, rather than translated through the larger context.

Translating this statement based on immediate context, you would think the Lord is saying, "In that day, you will not pray to Me, but only to the Father."

> **Now we are sure that You know all things, and have no need that anyone should question** (*erotao*) **You. By this we believe that You came forth from God.**
> **John 16:30 NKJV**

This is, of course, not accurate and is borne out by the following translations: *Matthew Henry Commentary, Vincent Word Studies, Expositor's Bible, Robertsons' Word Study, World Translation, Interpreter's Bible, Wuest, The Amplified Bible, Williams, Weymouth, W.E. Vine,* and many others.

The disciples must have understood Him to mean questions about where He came from and where He is going, because in Acts 1:6, they asked Him a question about the future kingdom, but they did not ask the questions that they asked Him in the Upper Room dialogue.

The thought of not praying to Jesus also is proven incorrect by the practice of the early Church which prayed on most occasions simply to God. As you study "The Acts of the Apostles," you will notice the absence of any models for prayer. This is important. It seems the scriptures are devoted to instructing the believer more about the commitment to a life of prayer than it is to teaching the forms of prayer.

Is it proper to pray to Jesus?

Can you pray to the Father?

Is there any circumstance in which one would pray to the Holy Spirit?

The scriptures are delightfully silent in dealing directly with these questions. However, the Bible is quite direct in dealing with the matter of prayer in the sense of its importance in the believer's life.

Jesus modeled a life of prayer throughout His life on earth. Peter and the first disciples appear to have given themselves to a disciplined schedule of prayer. In Paul's letters, he constantly refers to his prayer life.

While no instance gives credibility to any formula, here are the derived truths in simple, logical order:

1. Believers pray.

2. Believers pray regularly.

3. Believers pray about everything.

4. Believers pray to God.

It is acceptable to address God as "Lord," to pray to the Father, or to pray to the Lord Jesus, as in Acts 4:24, where He was addressed as the One Who created all things.

It is not acceptable to teach that prayers should not be offered to God except in some formula approach. When

New Testament scriptures are studied in the whole, there is no basis for teaching believers not to pray to the Father, nor is there biblical basis for teaching Christians not to pray to the Son.

God the Father, God the Son, and God the Holy Spirit are desirous of fellowship. As you grow in that fellowship, you will discover the rich diversity among the Trinity. On one occasion, you will hear what you understand to be the voice of the Father. On another, you will hear what you clearly understand to be the voice of the Son, the Lord Jesus. On yet a different occasion, you will hear what you know to be the voice of the Holy Spirit.

The story of Samuel is helpful at this point. He heard a voice calling out his name. The voice was so clear that he immediately thought it was Eli, the prophet with whom he had been sent to live. After several occurrences, Eli perceived that young Samuel was hearing the voice of the Lord God and instructed him on what to say.

In the beginning, most of us are like Samuel. We know we are hearing something. We just need time, and perhaps a little help, to develop our own heavenly communications system! Unfortunately, the Church of our era seems more intent on learning the technology of that system. Instead of placing emphasis on *what* is being communicated, they invest great energies in *how* it is being communicated.

*Give yourself to prayer. Do not give yourself to the formulas of prayer.*

Come to God in Spirit and in truth. If you will do this in integrity, you will stay out of ditches . . . and your prayer path will lead along a way that "grows brighter unto the coming day."

[This chapter was written by Dr. Roy Hicks Jr. just prior to his homegoing and is being printed posthumously.]

# 13

# Laughter

Little did I dream, when I wrote a book on laughter titled *He Who Laughs . . . Lasts, and Lasts, and Lasts* over fifteen years ago, that there would one day surface a need to write about excesses and a need for balance concerning this subject.

In the 70s, and farther back in Pentecostal circles, laughter was very often heard as congregations expressed their "joy in the Lord." They had an understanding of "a merry heart doeth good like a medicine."

One of the more popular choruses of the day was, "The Joy of the Lord is My Strength," and very often the worship leader would lead the congregation in laughter, set to the melody of the chorus!

I have personally led many congregations to rejoice before the Lord with the sounds of laughter. Why did I do this? Because the Bible commands God's people to do so!

Philippians 4:4 says, "Be rejoicing in the Lord always. Again I say, Be rejoicing." (Wuest, The New Testament, An Expanded Translation.) The Apostle Paul repeats this great admonition in 1 Thessalonians 5:16, "Always be rejoicing" (Wuest, *ibid.)*

In 2 Corinthians 9:7b, Paul admonishes us, **For God loveth a cheerful giver.** The Greek word translated cheerful here is *hilaros,* which is where we get our English word, hilarious.

The biblical questions raised by the current phenomenon of laughter breaking out during congregational worship is, "Is this a special move of the Holy Spirit that could be the last great move of God?" To avoid falling into a ditch, let's examine what the Bible has to say about "moves of the Spirit."

# The Holy Ghost Speaks of Jesus

An expression heard very often currently is, "Holy Ghost meetings," or people will say, "The Holy Spirit moved and we were all blessed, some were delivered and many laughed uncontrollably."

In the height of her ministry, Aimee Semple McPherson would conduct what she called Holy Ghost Rallies. Their purpose was to provide a time for believers to gather together and enjoy praising God and allowing the gifts of the Holy Spirit to operate.

Many people attending these meetings, who had not entered into this wonderful experience, would be gloriously filled with the Spirit. But always, even in a Holy Ghost Rally, Jesus was always exalted — not the Father or the Holy Spirit — but Jesus. After reading the twelfth chapter on petitioning, you can understand the importance of this.

If the current emphasis on the Holy Spirit was taught in the Apostle Paul's day, he would have said to the Corinthian Church, "For I determined not to know anything among you but the Holy Ghost." (Read 1 Corinthians 2:2.)

Whenever we cause emphasis to be placed on the Holy Spirit rather than on Jesus, it can sorely grieve the Holy Spirit. His mission is to teach of, lift up, and glorify Jesus in this earth. Is the present-day proclamation of the Holy Spirit changing this emphasis ?

Colossians 1:19 says, **For it pleased the Father that in Him** (Jesus) **should all fullness dwell**. In Colossians 2:9 we read, **For in Him** (Jesus) **dwelleth all the fullness of the Godhead bodily.** Colossians 1:12, 13 speaks of the Father **delivering** (transferring) **us from the power of darkness into the kingdom of His dear Son.** It pleases the Father and the Holy Spirit when we exalt the Lord Jesus Christ.

As you read this, you may ask "Is he saying that we should never pray to the Father?" No. We need to thank the Father for giving His only begotten Son to be our Saviour and bow our knee to Him in prayer as the Apostle Paul did in Ephesians 3:14.

Nevertheless, 2 Corinthians 1:20 teaches that all of the promises of God are in Him (Jesus). The disciples lifted up and preached Jesus Christ. The believers were martyred because of their faith in Jesus. Others **took knowledge of them, that they had been with Jesus** (Acts 4:13).

Does it not grieve the Holy Spirit to lift Him up and call attention to Him, rather than to Jesus? In John 16:7-16, Jesus taught us that the Holy Spirit would not speak of Himself but would reveal the truths of Jesus to us. This would include the Father God also, because Jesus taught that all that the Father had was His also.

We are not to talk about what the Holy Spirit is doing in order to magnify Jesus. We are to talk about Jesus, and as a result of that the Holy Spirit continually magnifies and makes the Lord Jesus and his Word real to us.

## Jesus Is the Word

While it is being taught, the Word of God is equal to Jesus Christ, the Incarnate Word, materializing on the platform and speaking to the congregation. If the saints are laughing so loudly that they cannot hear Him, would that not be grieving and quenching the Holy Spirit?

The Holy Spirit will always conduct services decently and in order. He will never cause people to laugh so loudly that others could not hear the precious Word of God being preached. Again, He will do this because He is to magnify Jesus.

But there is another very important reason the Holy Spirit will not disrupt the preaching and teaching of God's Word: the Word of God is what sets the captives free and keeps them free.

It is true that laughter and joy can release healing in the hearts of people, and a lack of joy can bring people into bondage. Moses taught Israel, **Because thou servedst not the Lord thy God with joyfulness and with gladness of heart for the abundance of all things: therefore thou shalt serve thine enemies** (Deuteronomy 28:47, 48).

However, Jesus said in John 8:31,32:

**If ye continue in my word, then are ye my disciples indeed;**

**And ye shall know the truth, and the truth shall make you free.**

In the New Covenant laughter is not the tool the Holy Spirit uses to set captives free. It is knowledge of the Lord Jesus through the teaching of the Word.

**The words (truths) that I have been speaking to you are spirit and life.**

**John 6:63 AMP**

Although our laughter will give us joy for the moment, it is the knowledge of God's **exceeding great and precious promises** (2 Peter 1:4) which transforms us into the image of Jesus Christ, thereby making us free. Laughter and joy open up the heart and mind to receive the Word which will set us free.

# The Holy Spirit Does Not
# Force You to Laugh

The Scriptures have already commanded us to rejoice always, not just when the Holy Spirit prompts us or when we feel like doing it. *Laughing in the Holy Spirit is as much a choice as speaking in tongues or paying tithes. It is not something the Holy Spirit makes us do.*

The Holy Spirit doesn't *make* anyone do anything. If you speak in tongues, you know that He gives the unction but you make the choice to act upon it. He is a gentleman. Satan is the one who tries to force people to do things.

Furthermore, if the Holy Spirit alone causes us to do what the Scripture has already commanded, then we should expect Him to make us pay our tithes, attend church, praise and worship, speak in tongues, and witness!

If we say we believe the Holy Spirit makes saints laugh, we would have to rewrite portions of the Bible! We are commanded to be joyful, which makes it our responsibility to initiate laughter, not the Holy Spirit's.

Spiritual joy is not an emotion, but a daily attitude of the heart. When the Apostle Paul said, "Rejoice in the Lord always," he spoke a continuous action command. We are to rejoice always, not just when we come together to sing and praise the Lord.

## Is Laughter Revival?

The Acts 2 account of the infilling of the Holy Spirit is used as proof by those who strongly encourage laughter to be a large part of their services that laughter is a valid sign of revival. The reference is to the fact that many thought the disciples were drunk at Pentecost, when they were only full of the new wine of the Holy Spirit. However, it is impossible to read into the Bible's description of the event any suggestion that the newly baptized disciples were laughing uncontrollably, because the amazement was not that they were acting drunk, but that they were speaking God's Word in languages that were foreign to them. If they were laughing uncontrollably, they could not have spoken.

The people of Jerusalem and all those who had come from around the world for Passover realized that they were witnessing something that was far more supernatural than laughter. The Gospel was being preached in their native tongues by unlearned men of Galilee!

Historically, laughter has never identified anyone as being spiritual, nor has it been the sign of revival. And if laughter, which is soulish, would usher in great revival, then that revival could not last anyway.

*Revival is always marked by the revelation of Jesus in the midst of His people.*

## Recognize and Correct Excesses

When Jesus is no longer lifted up and all believers talk about is the power of the Holy Spirit, familiar spirits can move in and cause attention to become focused on people and flesh. Very subtly, the focus of attention moves from knowing and becoming like Jesus to supernatural experience.

When this happens, we go to meetings not to glorify God and grow stronger in the Word to fulfill God's call on our lives, but just to have an experience. This is a fleshly attitude, which must be distinguished from the hungry heart who wants to become more intimate with the Lord.

The way you can detect this subtle change of focus from a godly hunger for God to a fleshly lust for supernatural experience is your attitude when you leave the meeting. Is your heart bursting with all God has imparted to you from His Word? Do you have a renewed passion for all He has called you to do? Or do you sigh that everyone in the Body of Christ is not experiencing what you are experiencing?

Another sure sign that what you are involved in has gone into a ditch is the form by which the "power" is manifested. Again, is laughter the focus of the service instead of Jesus, to the point that the Word is sacrificed? The Holy Spirit may do this from time to time, but always as an exception and not the rule.

How are the people acting during and after the service? Do they behave decently, or are they unruly and disorderly? There have been reports of believers barking and even vandalism after some meetings where laughter is emphasized. This is a definite warning that demon spirits are involved, because the Bible tells us that they cause people to act like animals and to become violent. (See Luke 8:27-33.)

Reports such as these should cause us to stop and go back to the foundations of our faith, to the Word of God, which is the only thing that can give us stability during great times of renewal and revival.

It is during these times that we will be faced with unfamiliar experiences, some of them of God and others which are not. Hebrews 4:12 tells us that only the Word of God can tell us the difference between what is of the spirit and what is of the flesh.

It is God's will that we always be open and receptive to the true manifestation of the Holy Spirit. He has nine gifts which He operates as He wills, not as the believer wills. Laughter is not mentioned among them. Again, we are commanded to rejoice and to have an attitude of joy. This is not something the Holy Spirit does to us or for us.

Pentecostals and Charismatics have always been perceived by evangelicals and other denominations as being emotionally unstable and living by emotional experiences instead of God's Word. I do not believe this is a true statement, but there are times when we make great contributions to their conclusions!

A paraphrase of Ephesians 5:18-21 could read thusly: "Stop being drunk, or intoxicated with wine or acting like those that do get drunk. But be continually under control (by the Spirit). At all times be speaking continually to one another and to your own self in Psalms, the Word, and hymns that are about the Word." Satan will always be endeavoring to take us away from the truth. Jesus is truth and so is the Word.

People stray from sound doctrine, particularly the revelation of Jesus Christ, and become cults. Then they tend to resist adjustment or change. The first step back to balance is to begin to exalt the Lord Jesus Christ and His precious Word. Do not allow the flesh or soulish exxperiences to control. Make room for pure worship in the Spirit and room for the Word to go forth in an orderly manner, without confusion. Remember Psalms 55:19b, "Because they have no changes (change of course) there is no fear of God in them".

When the movement of laughter we are seeing today has been criticized, the admonition of Gamaliel to the Sanhedrin has been quoted many times as a warning that one could be found to be fighting against God, which could certainly be true.

The Jews of that day had witnessed a mighty miracle when the lame man was healed and they saw him leaping and walking and praising God. It was absolute physical proof of the power of God, not a manifestation of questionable demonstration of the flesh.

Gamaliel's warning was contrasting the work of God and the work of man. He did not refer to or know about the work of Satan. He omitted any reference to him inasmuch as he had no teaching or experience concerning him.

Now, because we have the written Word, we know that Satan can appear as an angel of light to accomplish his evil purpose. We know he can bring in another Gospel and cause saints to be deceived and end up in great error. (See Galatians 1:6.)

Many voices today give great latitude concerning the occurrence of signs and wonders that were promised in the last days. We must remember that we are not to be gullible and receive just any supernatural manifestation as from God, but "try the spirits." (1 John 4:1.)

And let us not be running from meeting to meeting and church to church trying to experience the supernatural. If we paraphrase the words of Jesus in John 4:48, it would be a strong rebuke. "What's wrong with you people! Unless you are always seeing signs and wonders, you stop believing!"

The Word is what brings faith (Romans 10:17.) and stability (Isaiah 33:6). I have noticed that when there is a lack of teaching, Christians tend to become experience-oriented instead of Word-oriented, and their lives reflect this lack of faith and stability. Remember, we are not destroyed or lose what we have for lack of laughter, but for the lack of knowledge. (See Isaiah 4:6; Hosea 4:6.)

You will be saved from many disappointments if you will remember *to judge experience by the Word, not the Word by experience.* Those believers who put the Word first in their lives and seek Jesus above all else remain stable and strong in the joy of the Lord.

# Conclusion:
# Balance Means Staying
# in the Center

My prayer for each reader is that he or she will have discovered this truth through reading the foregoing pages: It is through much effort that the Church of Jesus Christ will remain in balance. We must hold onto what is good and biblically sound. Yet we must always be ready to accept changes in our traditions and interpretations as the Holy Spirit reveals to us things that are "off-center." The psalmist stressed this in Psalm 55:19, **Because they have no changes, therefore they fear not God.**

Perhaps it will help you to have a brief summary of each of the previous thirteen chapters to recognize the "ditches" discussed in these pages.

### Spiritual Gifts:

Extremes range from the belief that they are not in operation at all today to the acceptance of anything supernatural as being of God. Either extreme can grieve the Holy Spirit. Only through strong, careful direction by church leadership can the gifts of the Holy Spirit operate decently and in order within our services.

### The Trinity:

Almost all cults may be recognized by their mistreatment of the trinity. To stay out of "ditches," the Godhead must always be presented exactly as They are: co-equal, co-eternal, co-omniscient, and co-omnipotent.

Throughout Scripture, where the term God is used, it clearly expresses the union and agreement of the Godhead.

### Faith:

Simply put, the "faith message" is that God is a good' God who desires to bless you in all areas of your life. If you will renew your mind with His Word, believe His promises, confess them as yours, and act upon them, His blessings will be yours. The ditch to avoid is believing and confessing things that are your own idea and not found in God's Word.

### Suffering Saints:

Saints have always suffered. Suffering comes because you are in the will of God and the devil is trying to stop you or because you are out of the will of God and have opened the door to the devil through sin. True "saints" did not blame God for their suffering, and to stay out of a ditch, you must not either.

### Intercession:

Matthew 18:18 tells us that we can bind or stop satanic activity, but it does not tell us that we can "bind" the will of another. We cannot keep Satan from ruling this world system, but we can bind him and pray God's Word and will into the earth. *All* saints are called to be intercessors, available for this work at all times.

### Divorce and Remarriage:

Divorce and remarriage are not unpardonable sins. Even if you caused your divorce, as a Christian you can be forgiven. If we hold the past sins of Christians against them, we put them in unscriptural bondage. The New Covenant is one of love, and love never makes room for sin or unforgiveness.

### Hero Worship:

History is full of many examples that show clearly how humans always seek someone to put on a pedestal, someone to follow. The world idolizes movie stars and athletes; believers many times idolize pastors, television evangelists, or prophets. They have the idea that these men and women are infallible. Hero worship of a man or woman leads to confusion and discouragement. Christians should only have one hero, and His name is Jesus!

### Praise and Worship:

As born-again believers, we worship God in spirit and in truth. We praise and thank Him for His Word and by His Word, and we worship Him through the power of the Holy Spirit within us. Praise and worship are a lifestyle, not just something we do on Sundays.

### Prosperity:

Wealth is not a measure of spirituality, and the love of it is the root of all evil. However, prosperity is not just money. Prosperity is very plainly taught in many verses of Scripture and is simply receiving the manifold blessings of the Lord as you seek first the kingdom of God and His righteousness. The purpose of prosperity is to take the gospel to the world.

### Eschatology:

Some views are extremely spiritualized and others are extremely literalized. One ditch says, "I do not believe Christ will return in my lifetime," while the other ditch is busy setting dates of His imminent return. The balance comes in emphasizing that being ready to meet Him is far more important than trying to anticipate *when* He will come. The time has been pre-set by God, and no one in the Church or their works will influence the time of His coming. We simply are instructed "to be ready."

### Prophets:

New Testament believers are primarily led by the Word of God and the indwelling Holy Spirit. God will speak words of wisdom, knowledge, and prophecy as He wills. We are to beware of false prophets and recognize them by their fruit. We seek the counsel and confirmation of those wise in the Word of God and strong in the Holy Spirit, not fortune tellers who are moved by familiar spirits.

### Petitioning:

I pray that Chapter 12, written by my late son, Pastor Roy Hicks Jr., will help not only all those who read it but all who are interested in doing their own studies of this all-important subject. Roy Jr. was totally correct when he showed us clearly that formulas or principles of prayer are not as important as the attitude of the heart and living a life of prayer.

### Laughter:

The Bible commands us to be cheerful and have an attitude of joy because the joy of the Lord is our strength. The Holy Spirit does not make us laugh, although there can be times of tremendous laughter when believers come together in worship. This laughter can bring great healing and health to an individual, but it is the Word of God that makes us free and keeps us free. In times of revival, many supernatural experiences will occur; only the knowledge of God's Word will keep you from falling into ditches.

### A Final Word:

Balance means staying in the center of the Word of God and listening to the Holy Spirit, which will keep you from getting off into ditches to the left or right through tradition, men's interpretations, or vain imaginations.

You can maintain this balance by being involved in a church where the Word of God is taught and the Holy Spirit is allowed to move. It is in this healthy and loving environment, rubbing elbows with other saints who will encourage you and whom you will encourage, that you become a doer of the Word and grow up in the knowledge and experience of God.

Why? So you will be equipped by God to go out and be salt and light to a lost and dying world!

**Roy H. Hicks** is a successful minister of the Gospel who has given his life to pastoring and pioneering churches throughout the United States. He has served the Lord in various foreign fields, having made missionary journeys to South America, the Orient, Australia, and New Zealand.

Dr. Hicks formerly served as General Supervisor of the Foursquare Gospel Churches and has become a popular speaker at charismatic conferences.

Perhaps the thing that most endears Dr. Hicks to readers is his warmth and his ability to reach out as the true believer he is — a man of strong, positive faith, sharing a refreshing ministry through the power and anointing of the Holy Spirit.

To contact Dr. Hicks,
write:
Dr. Roy H. Hicks
P. O. Box 4113
San Marcos, California 92069

*Please include your prayer requests
and comments when you write.*

# Books by Dr. Roy H. Hicks

## The Harrison House Vision

Proclaiming the truth and the power
Of the Gospel of Jesus Christ
With excellence;

Challenging Christians to
Live victoriously,
Grow spiritually,
Know God intimately.